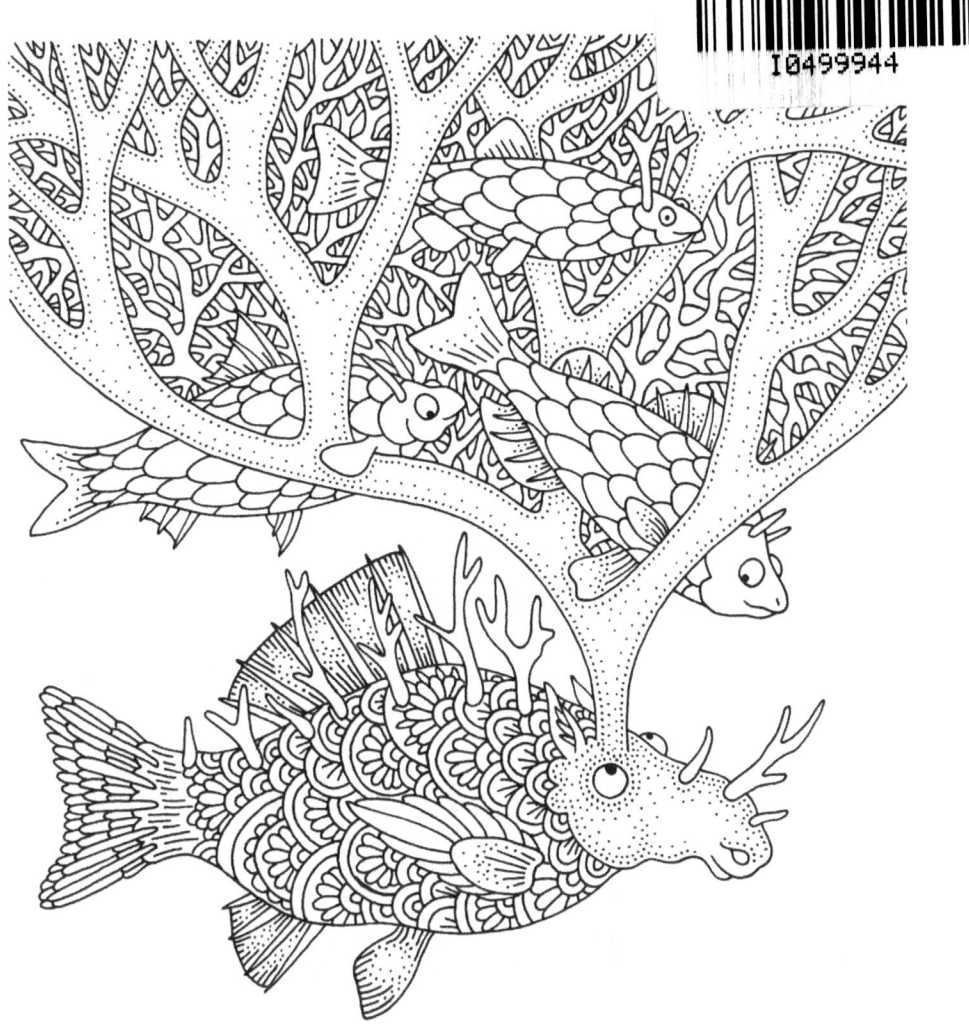

This book belongs to

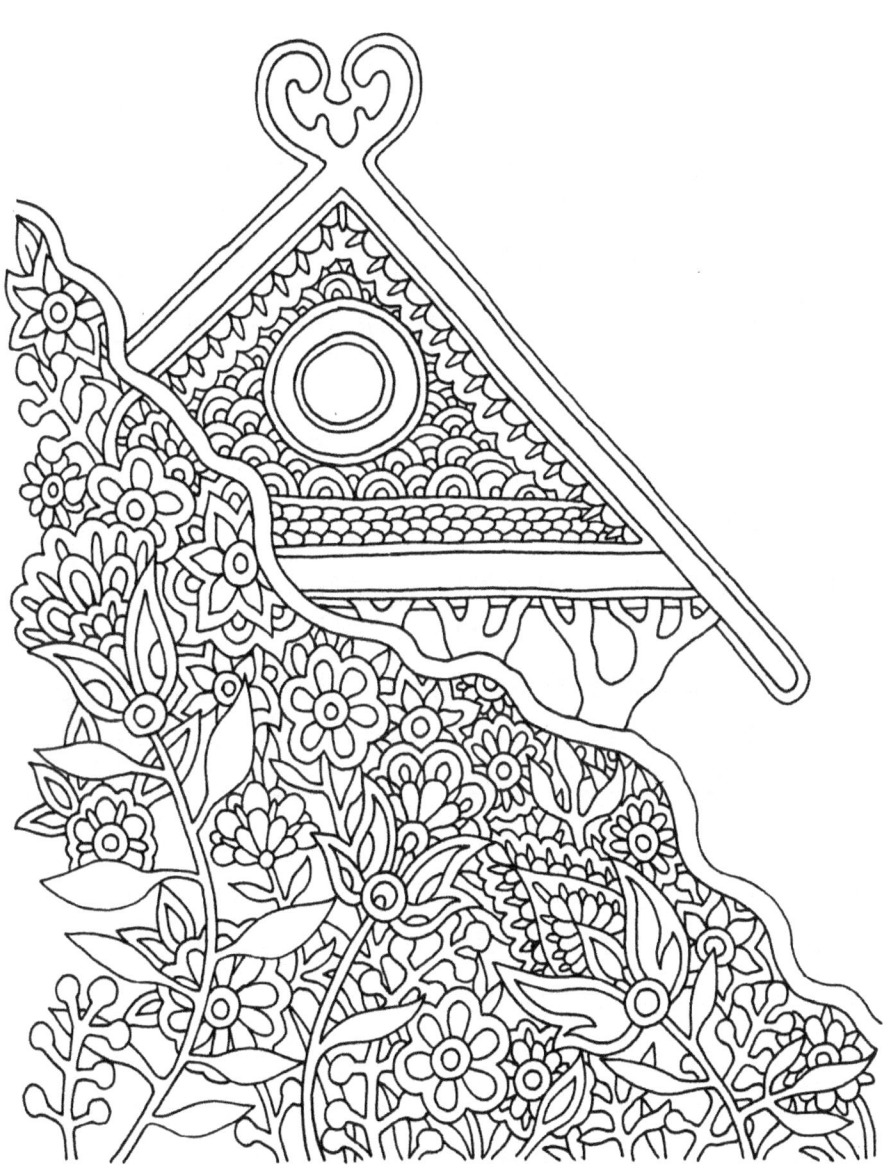

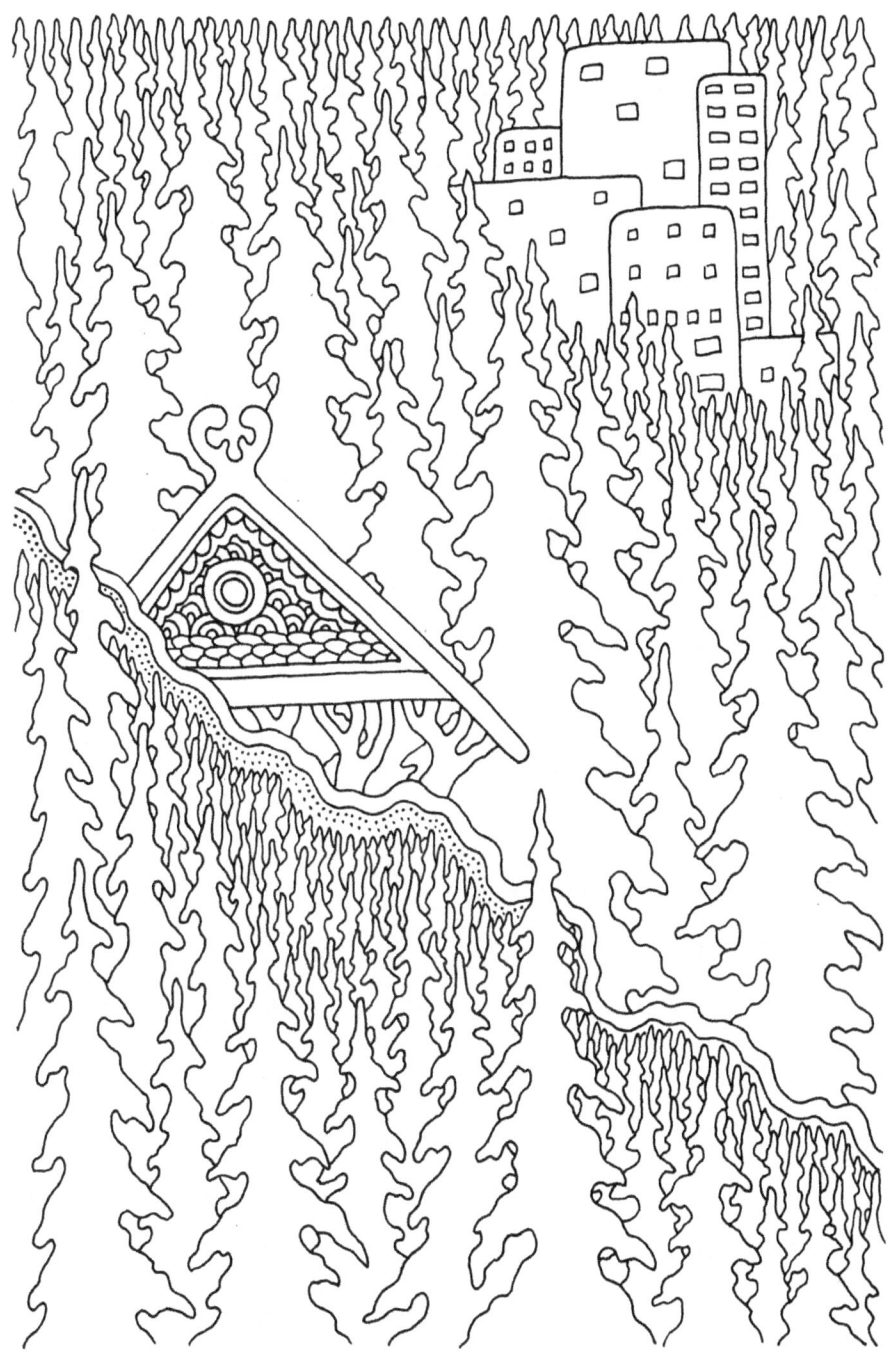

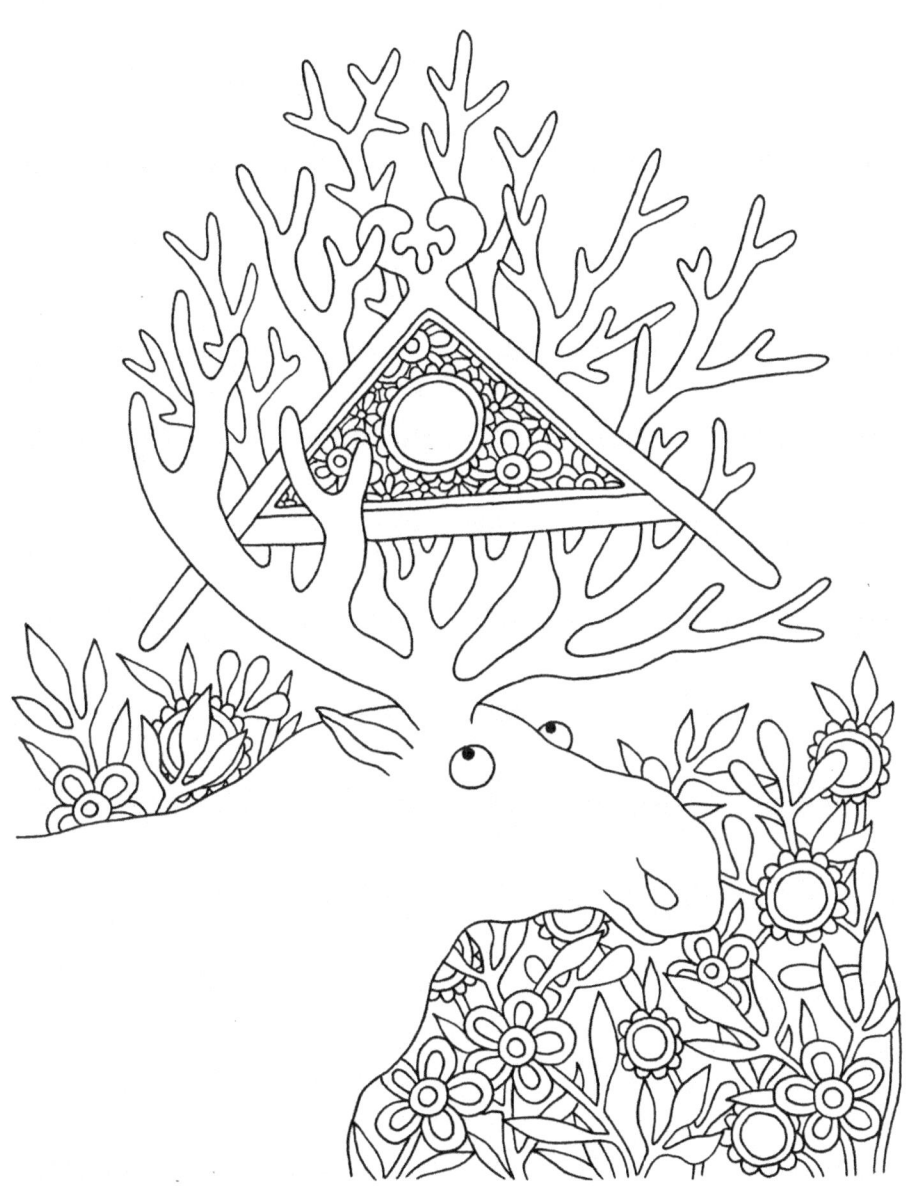

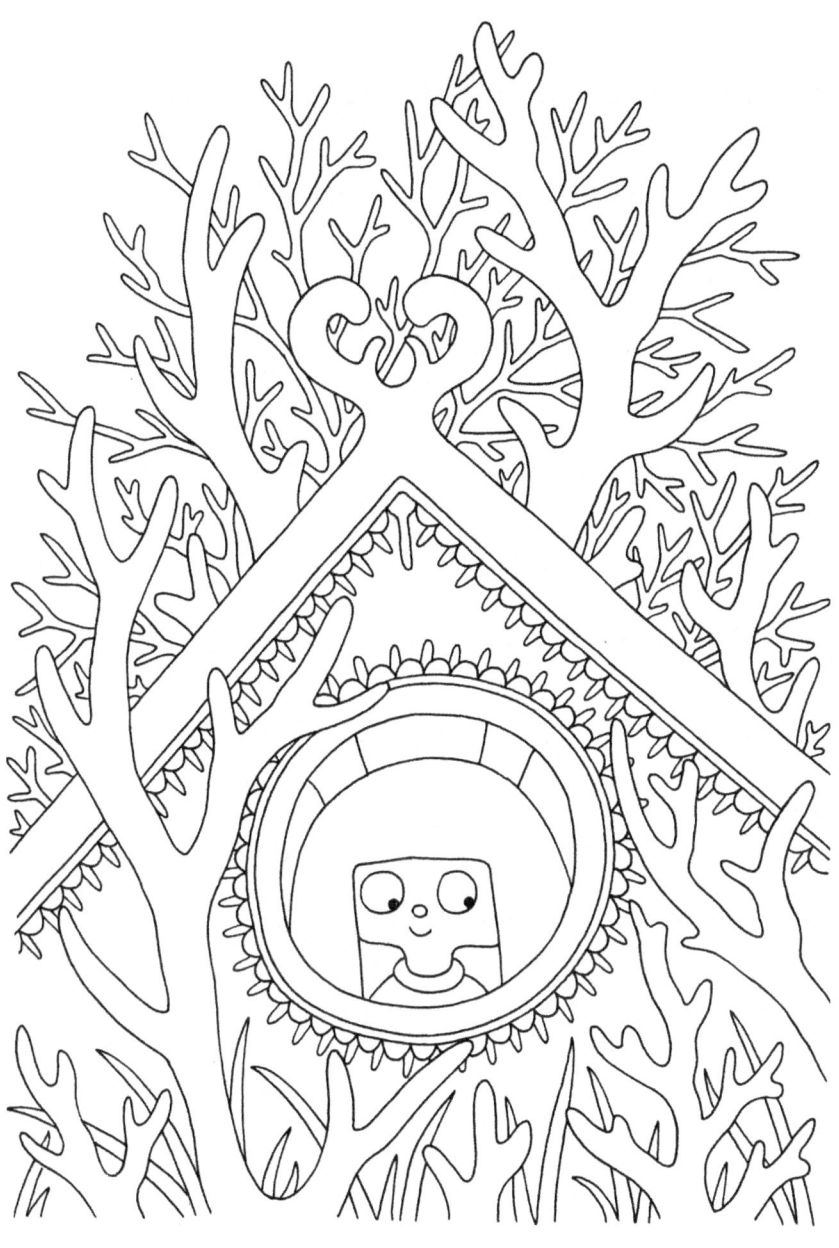

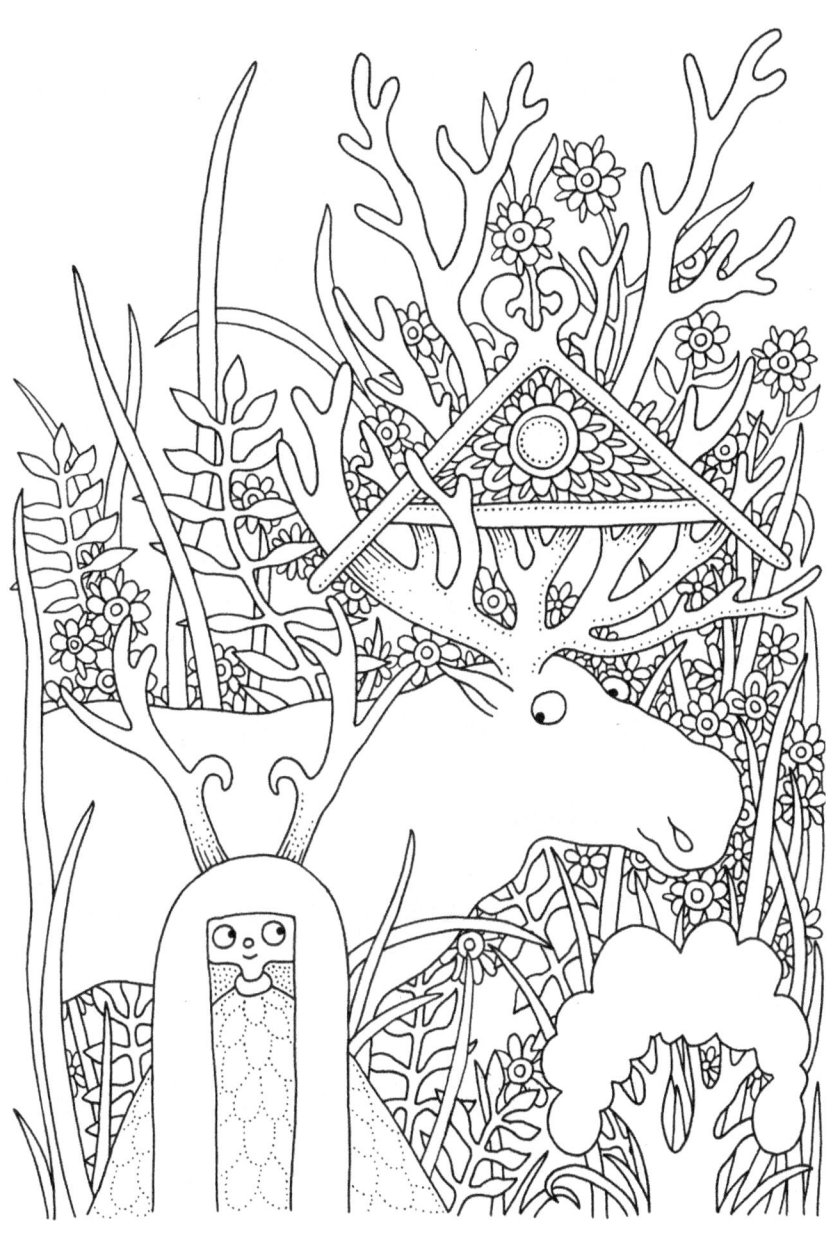

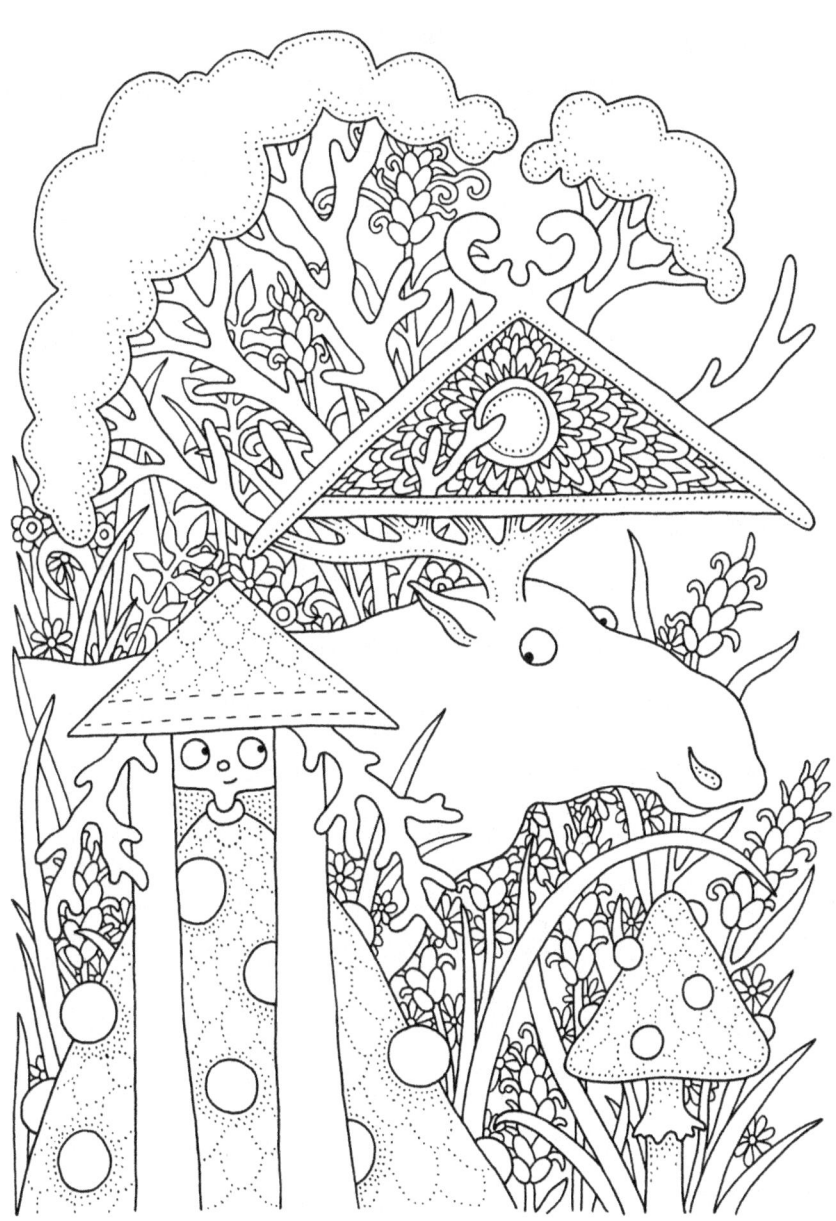

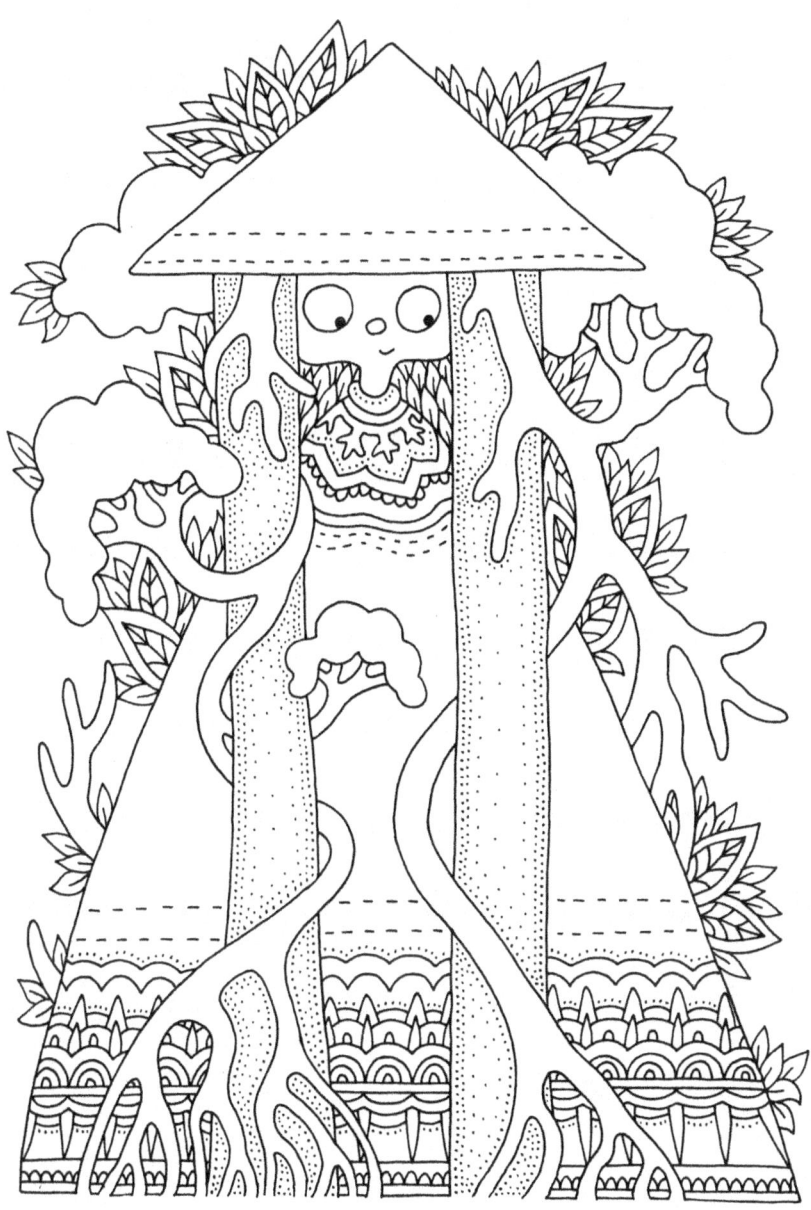

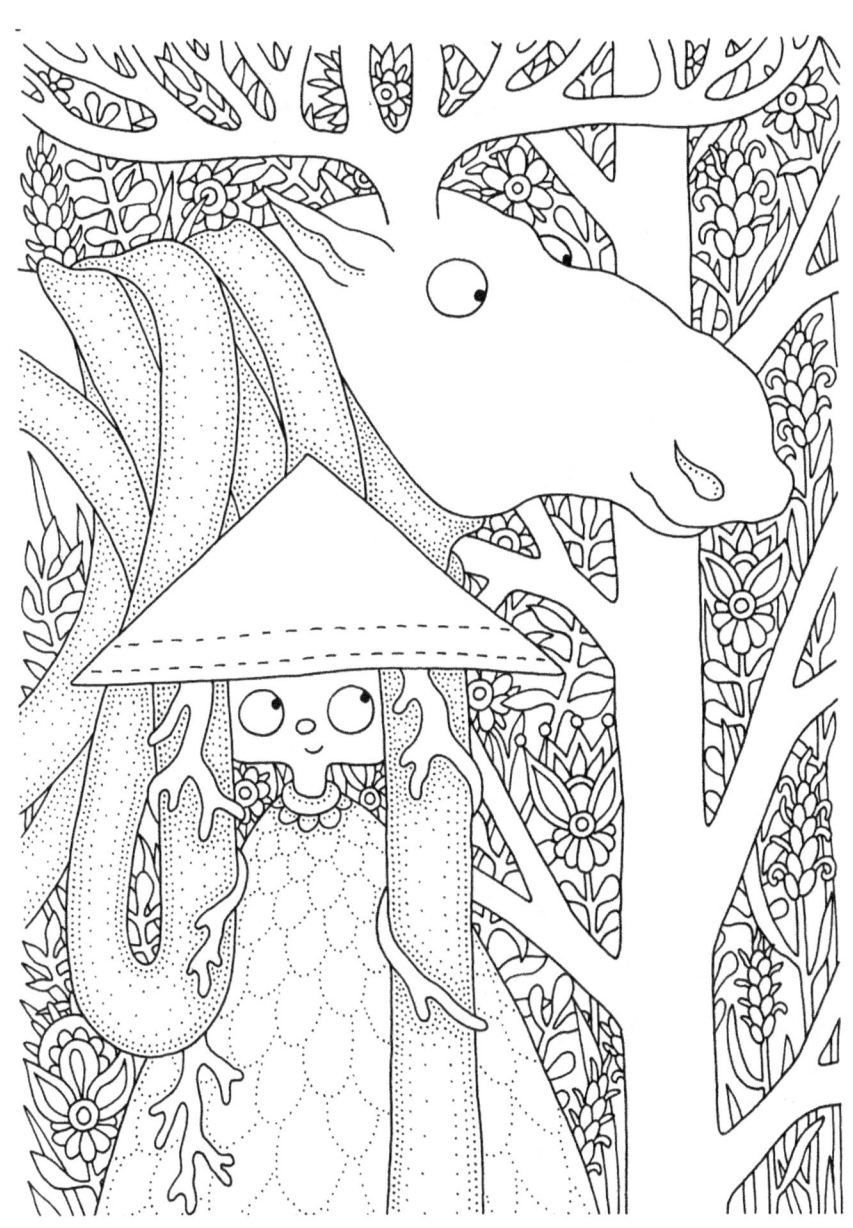

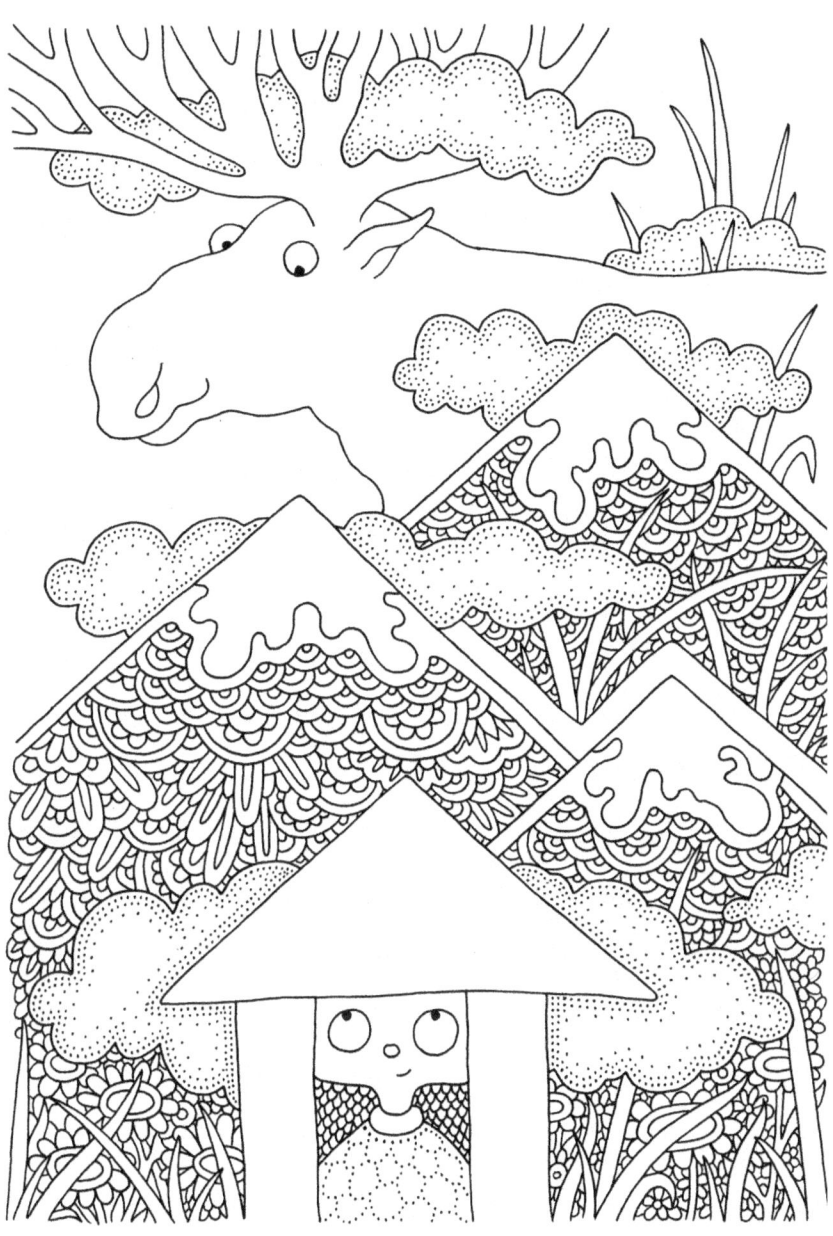

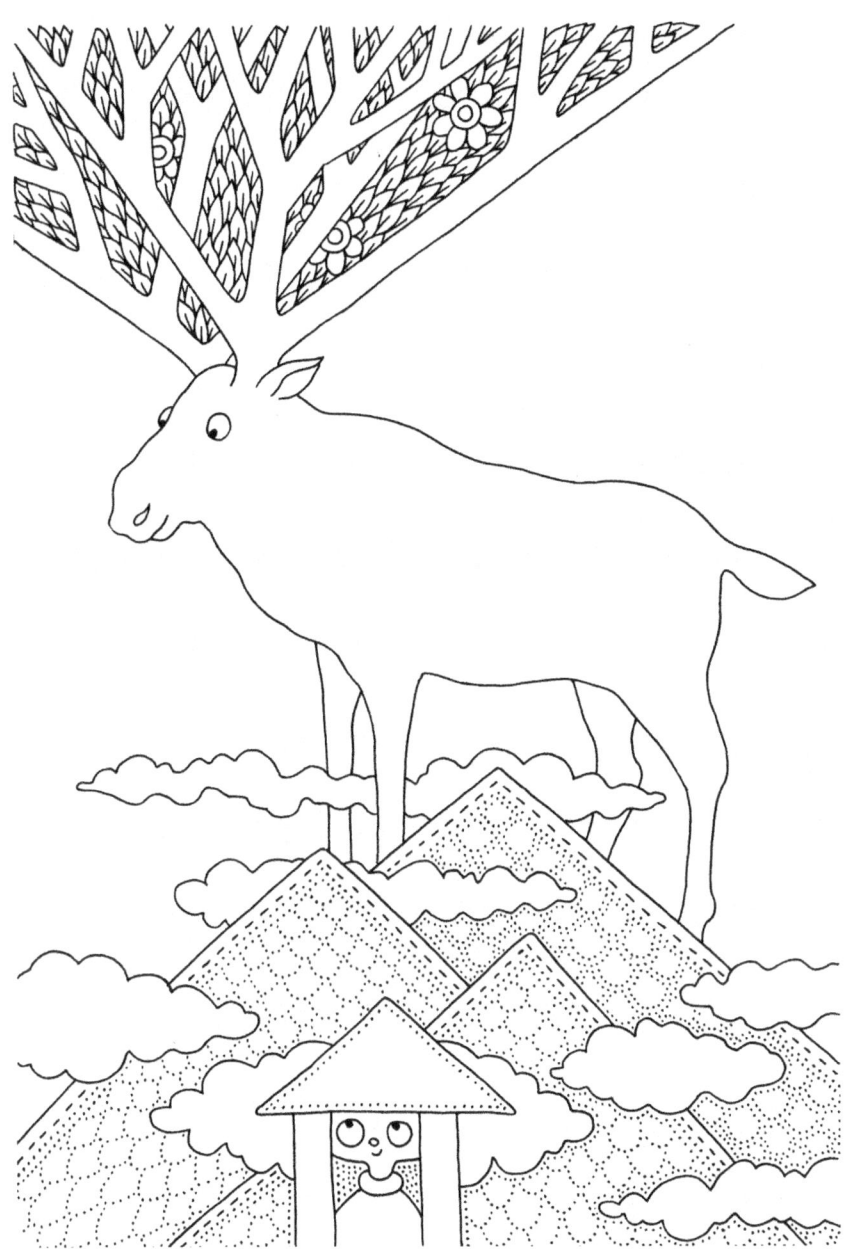

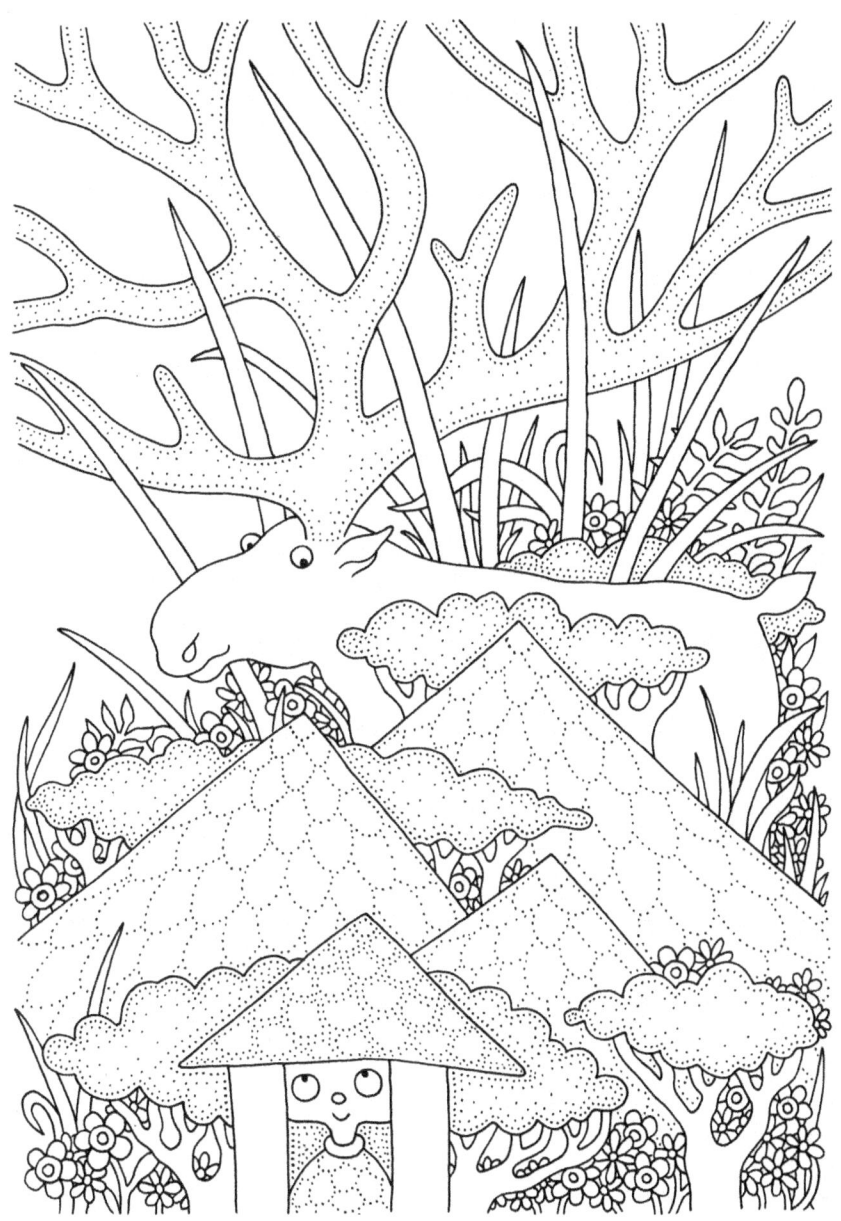

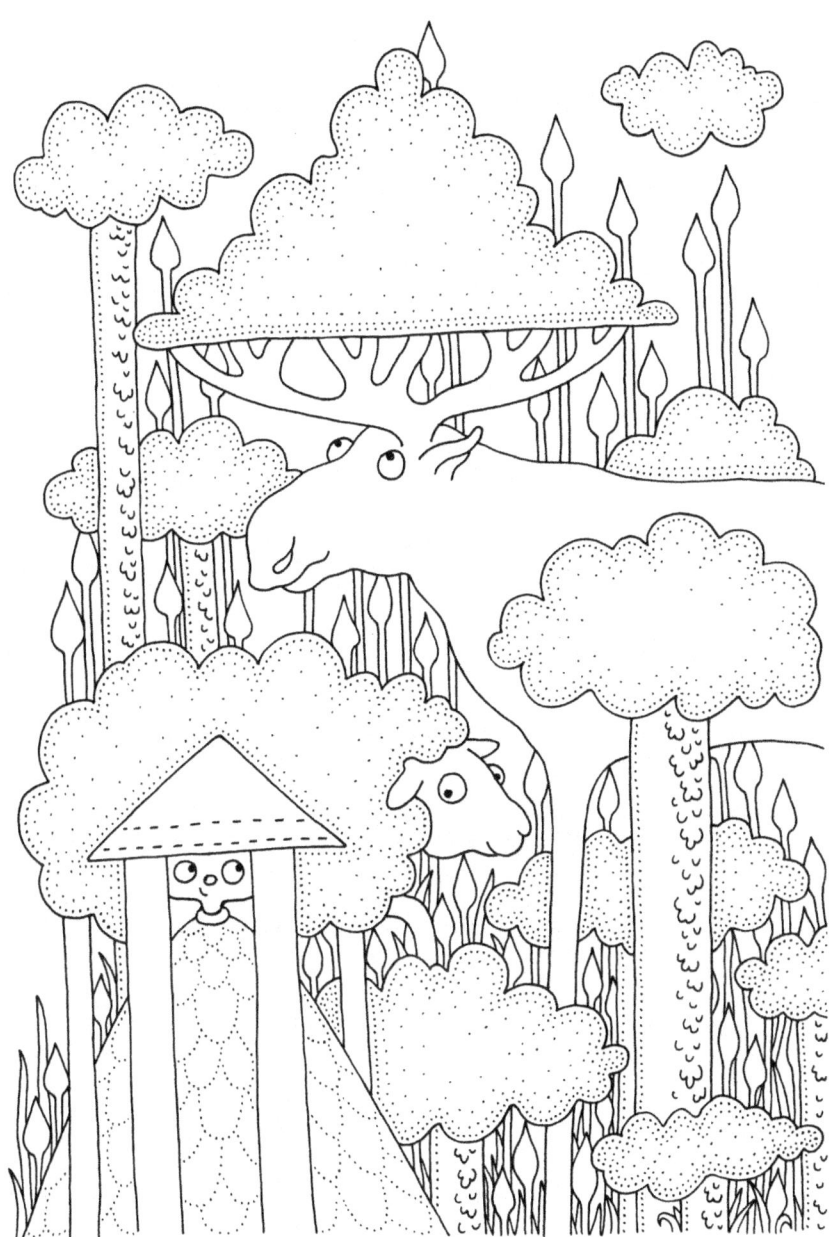

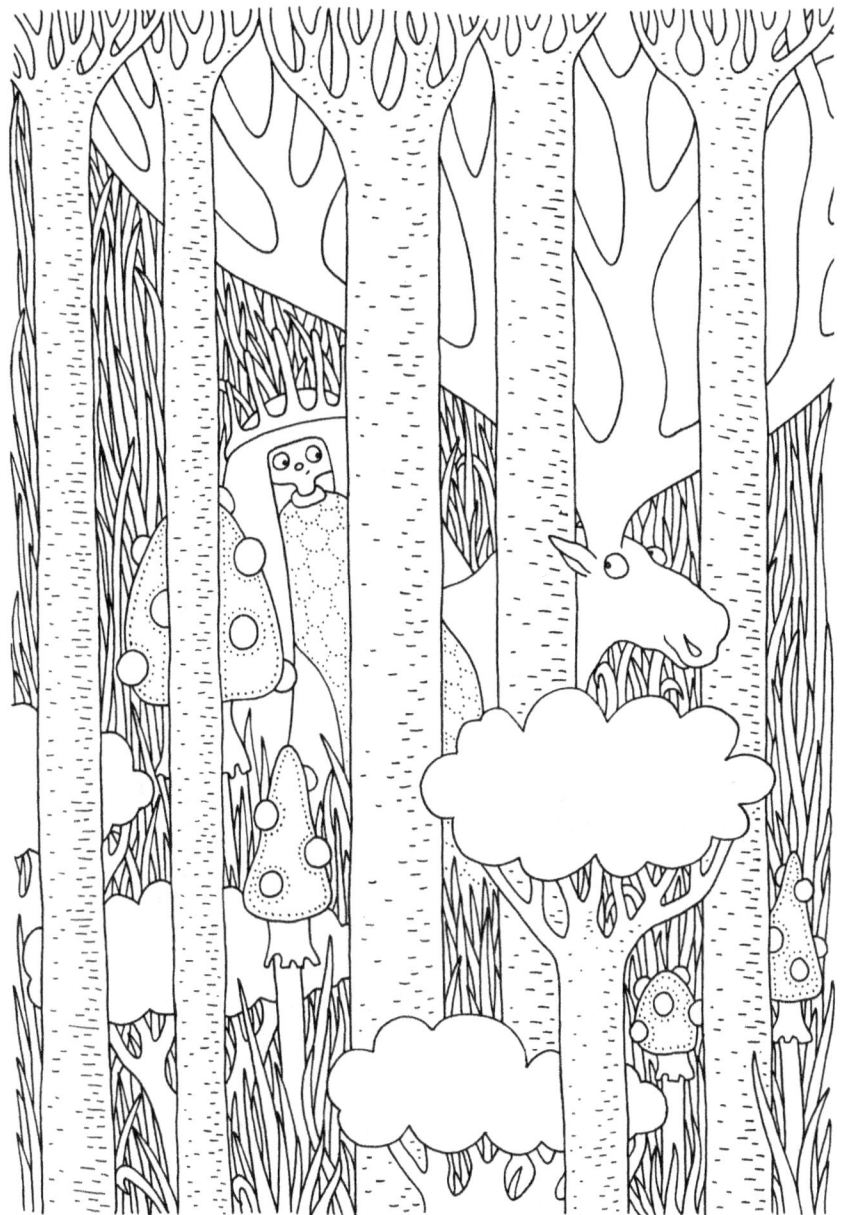

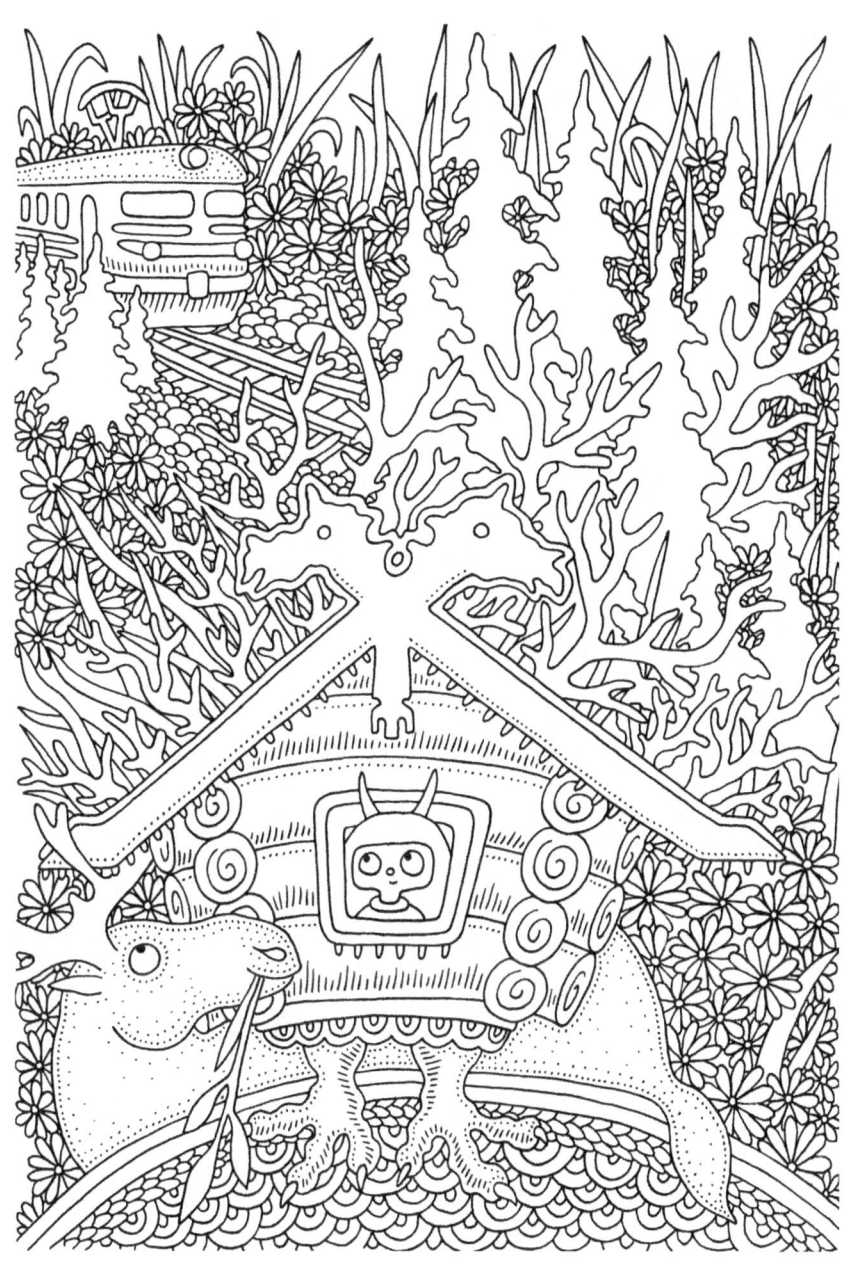

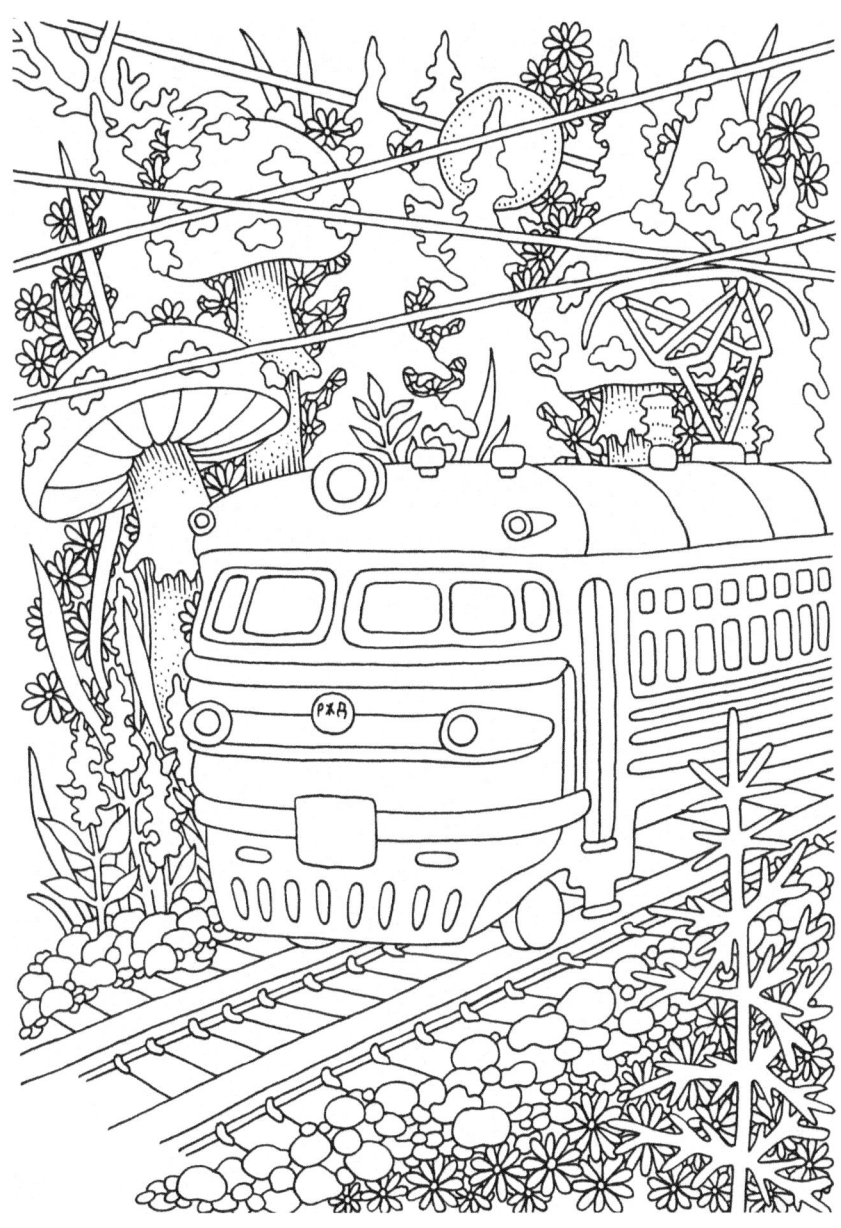

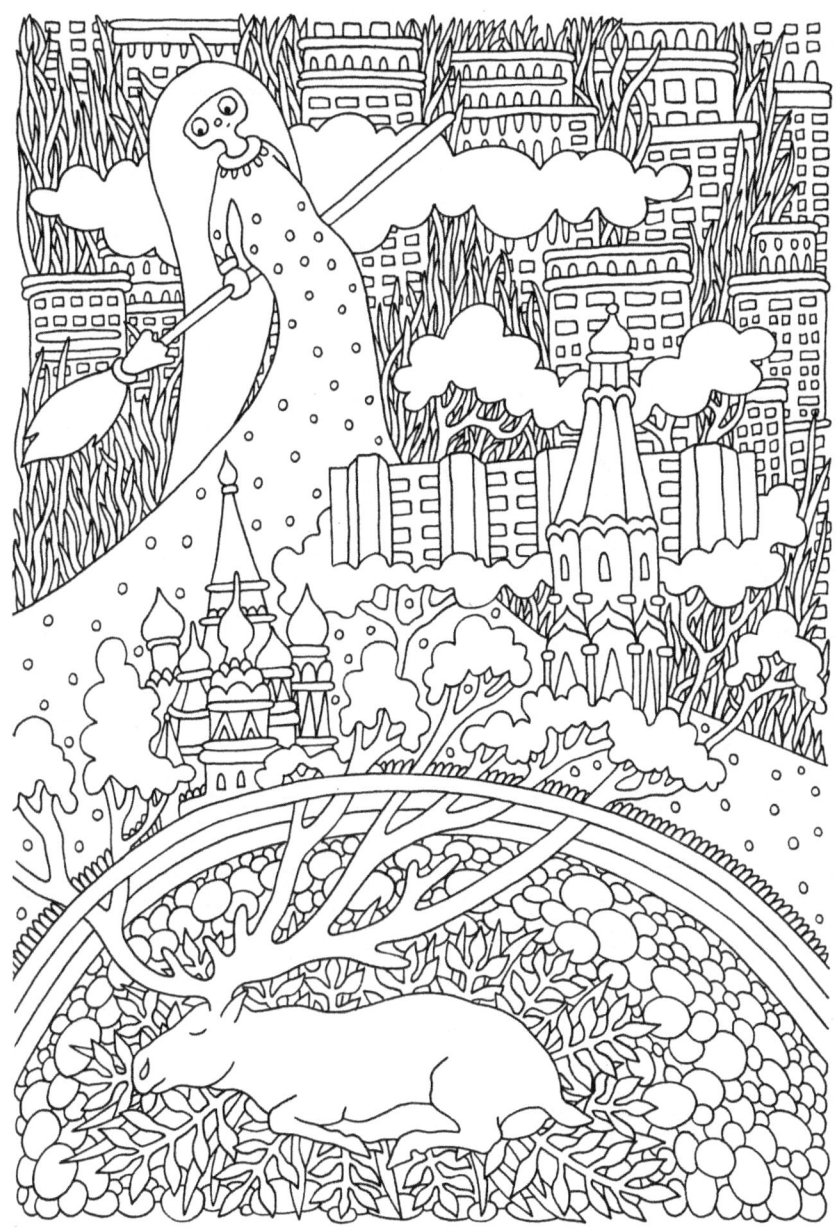

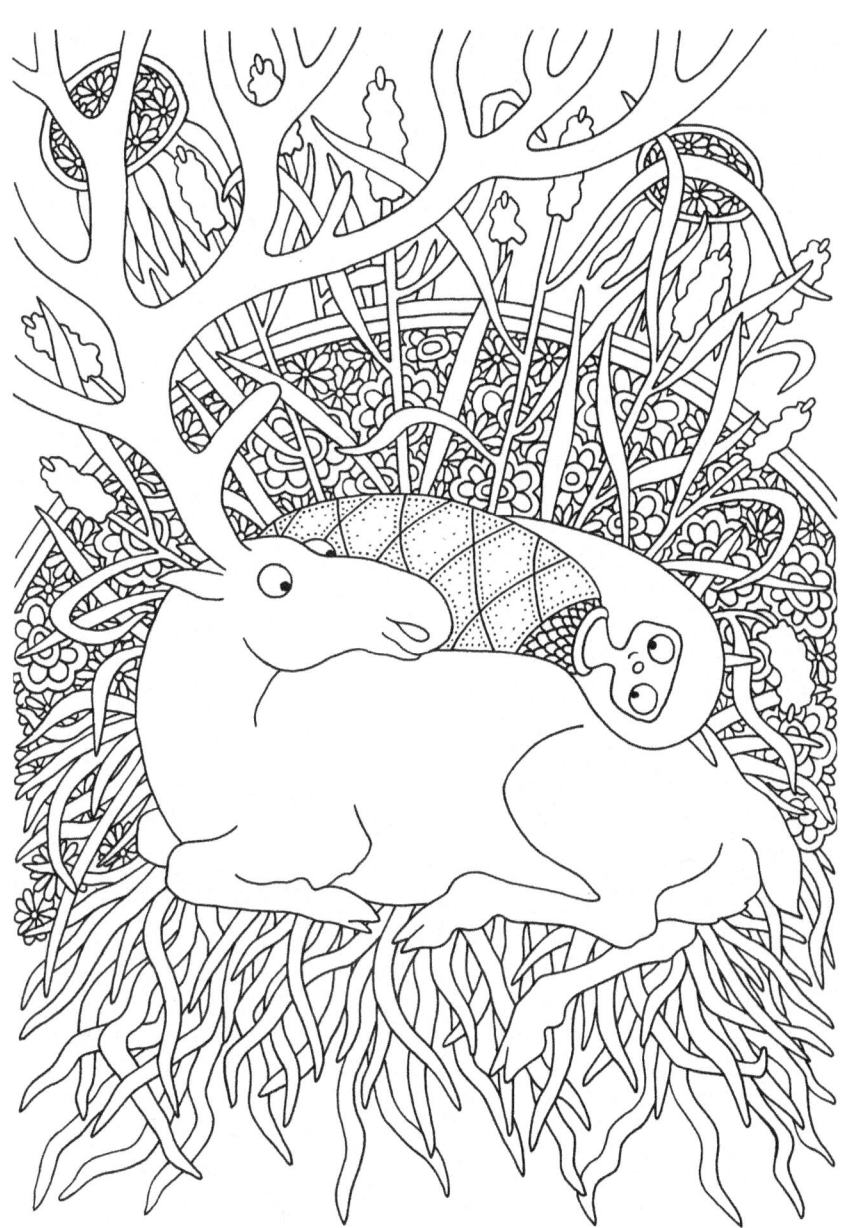

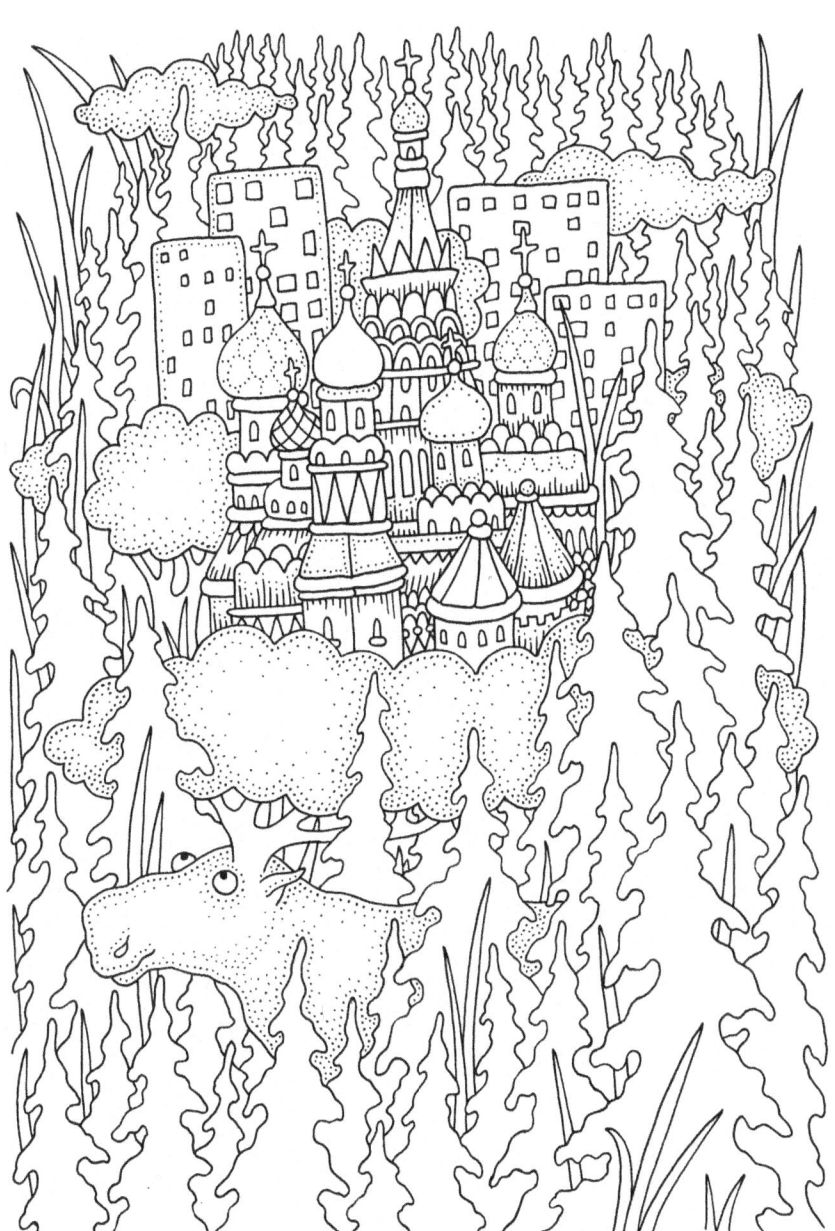

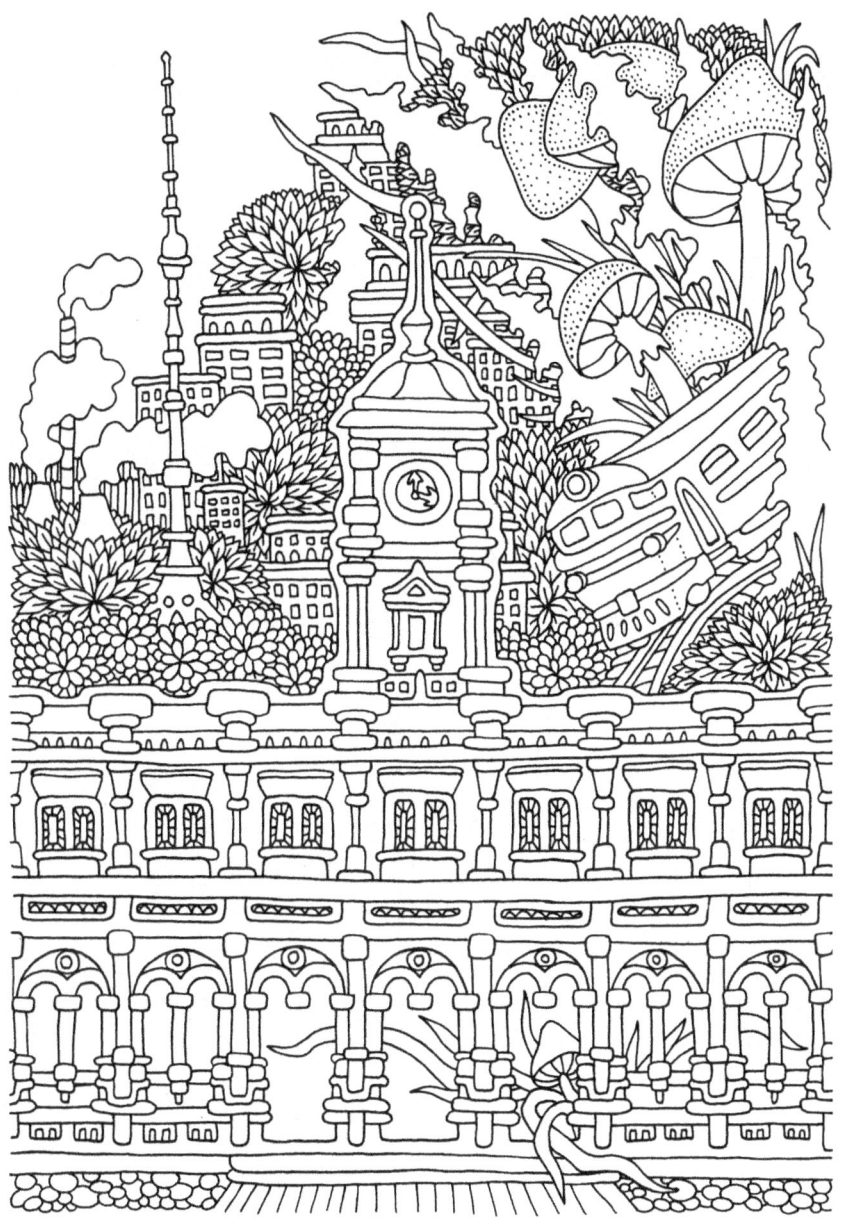

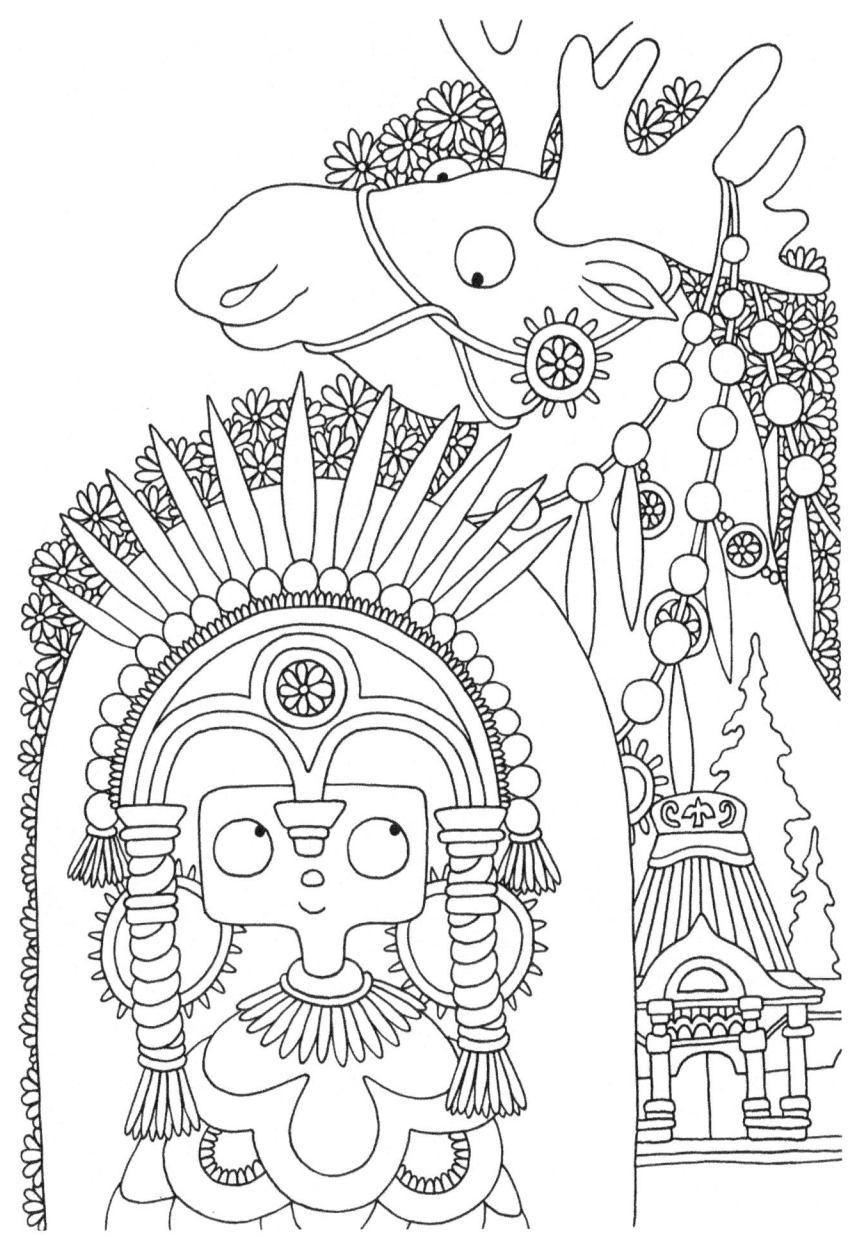

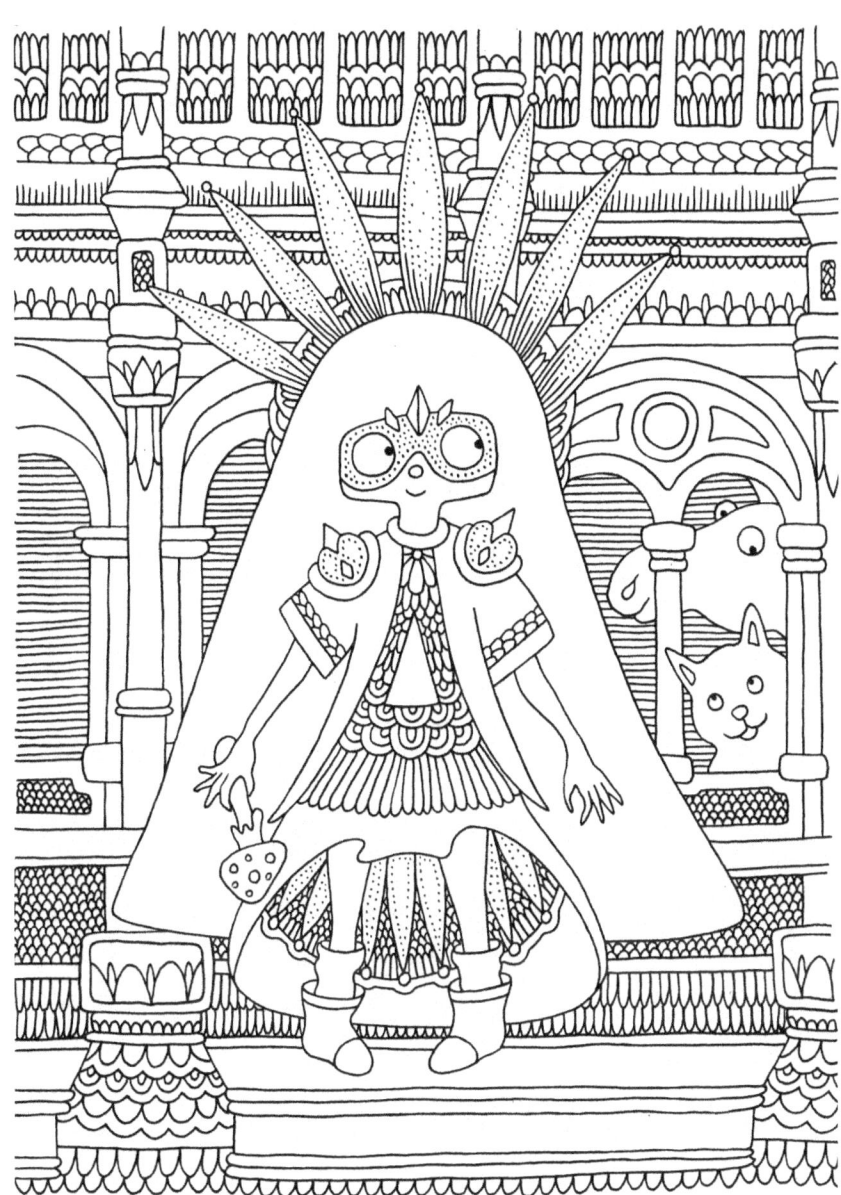

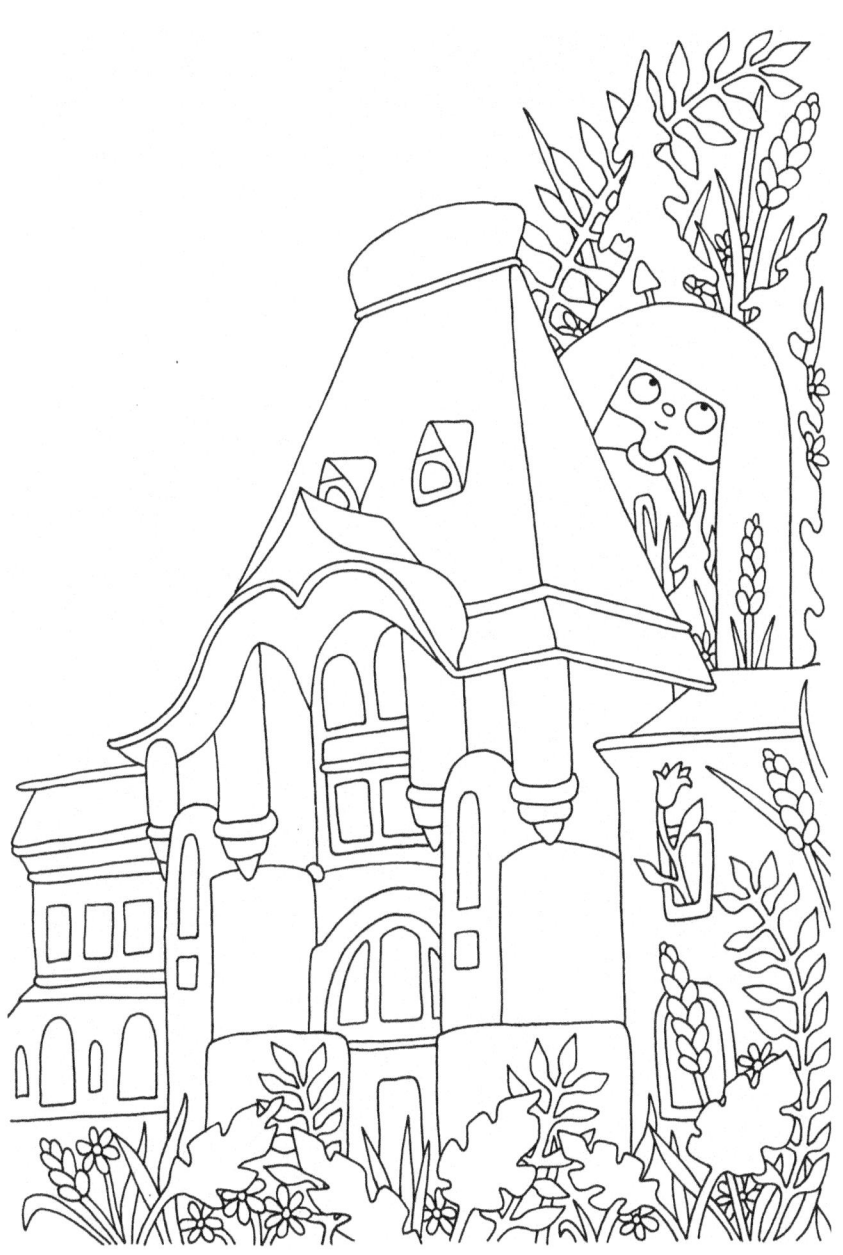

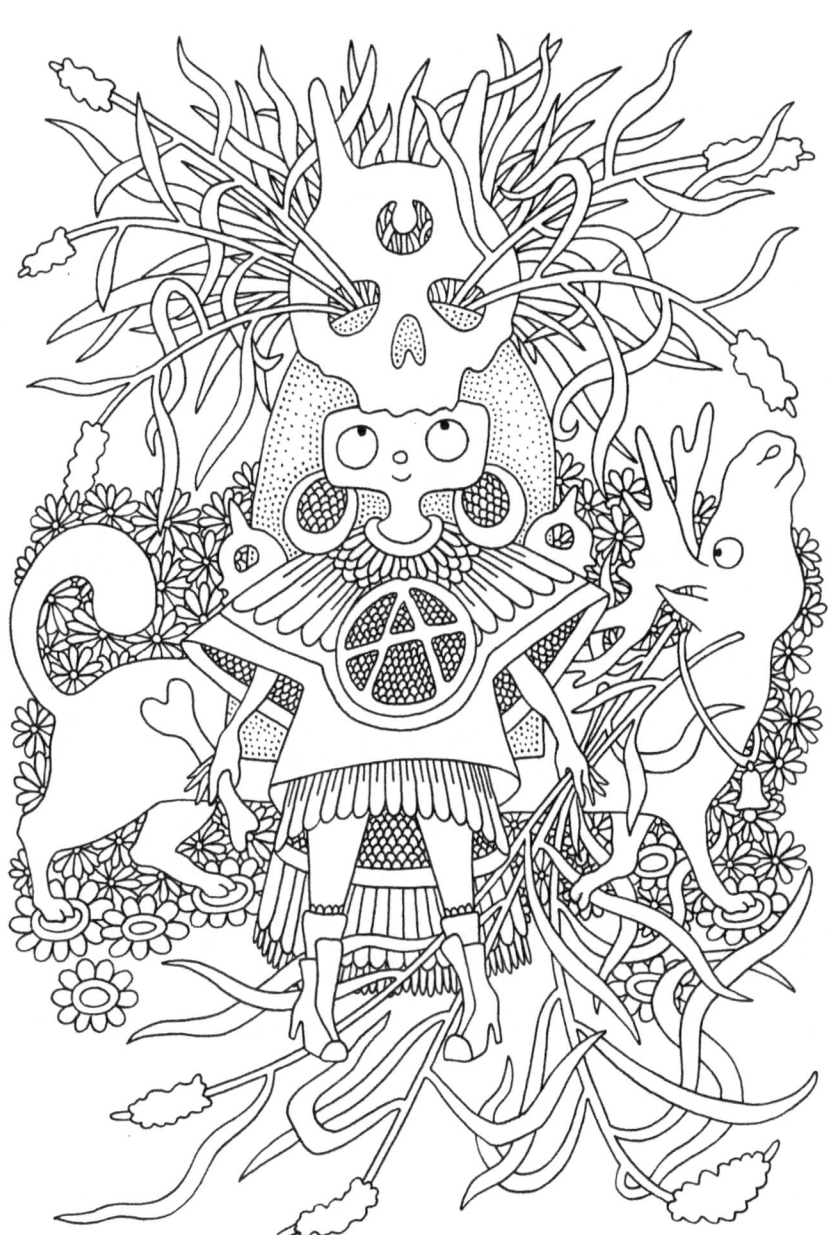

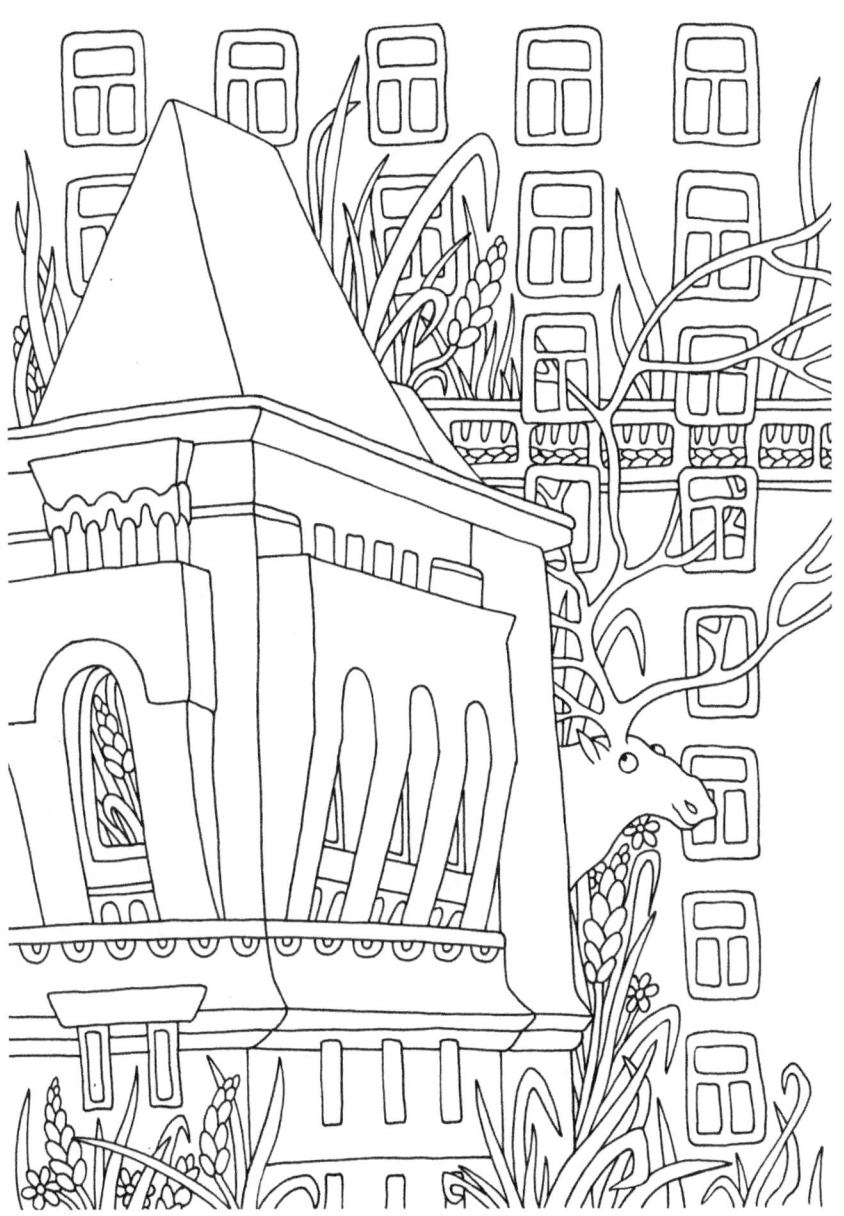

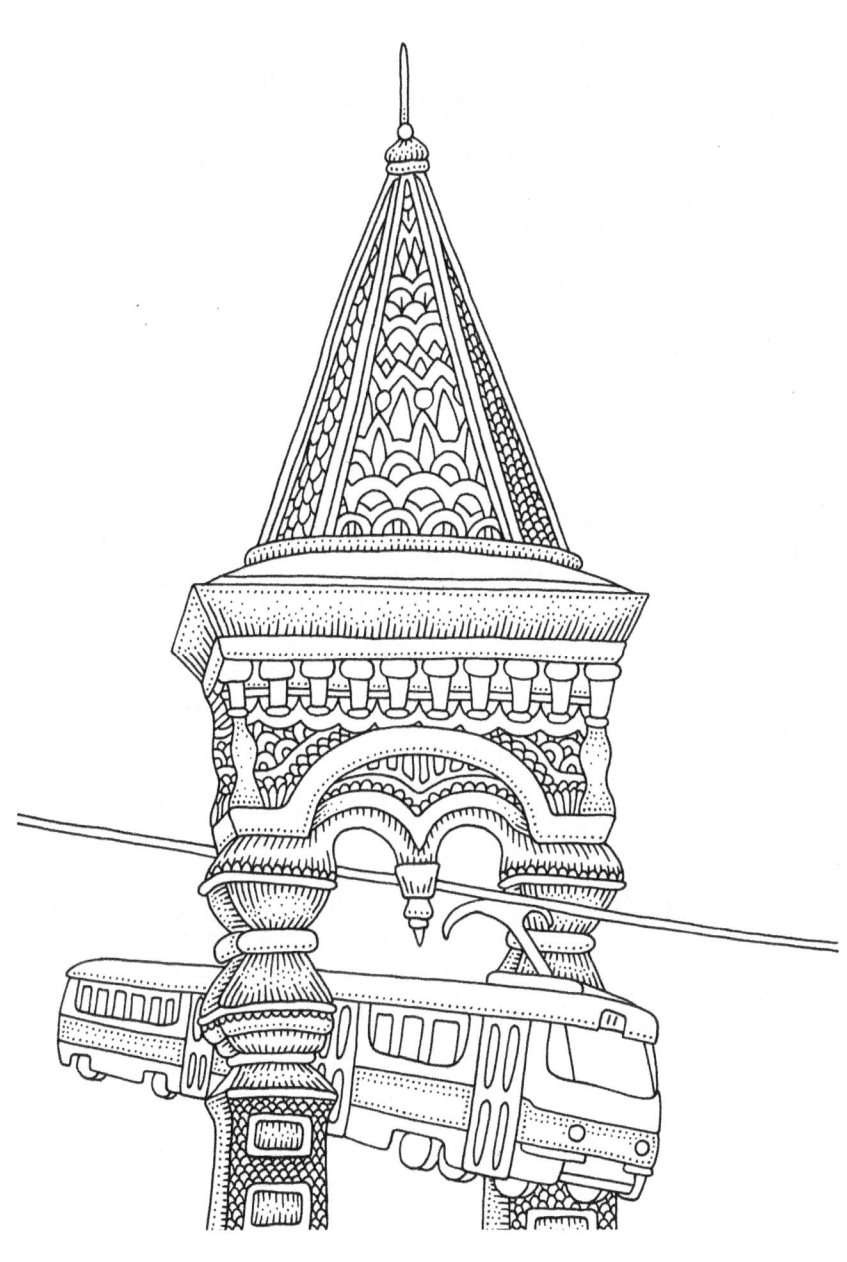

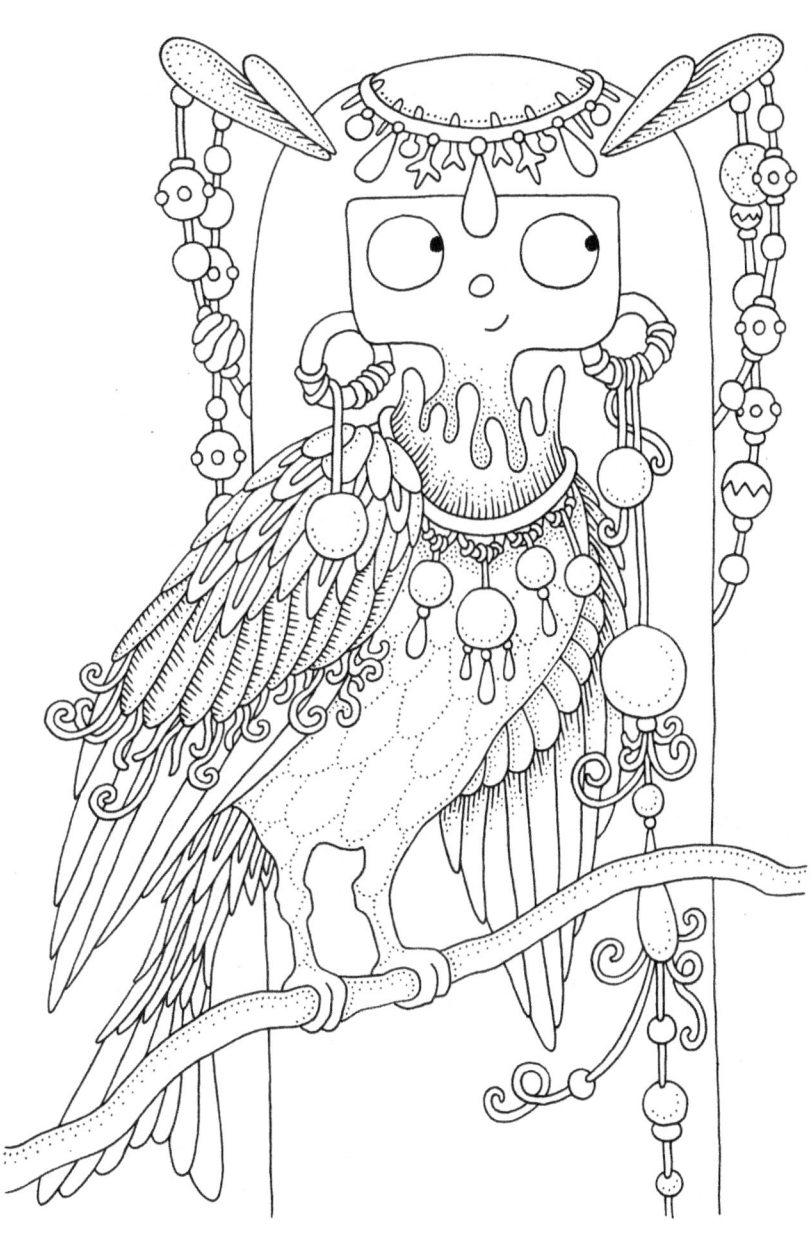

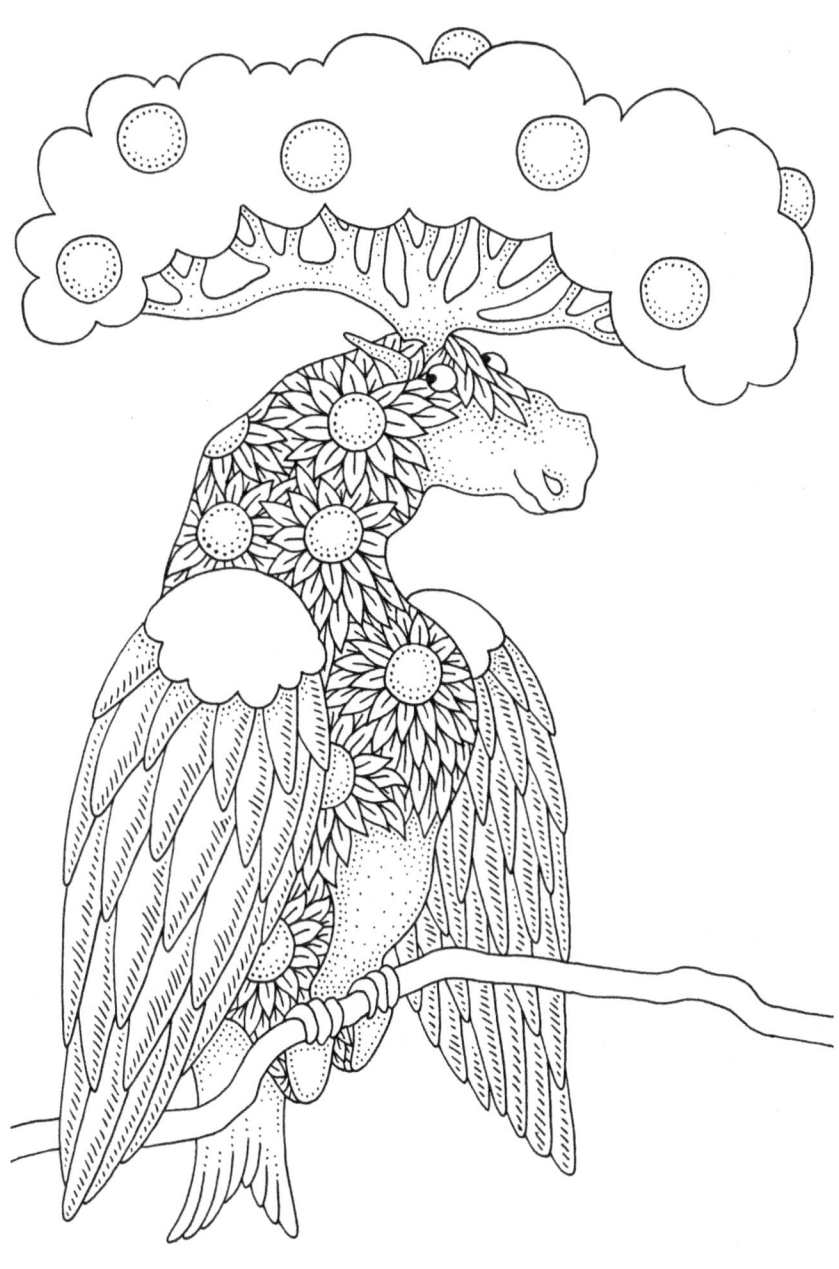

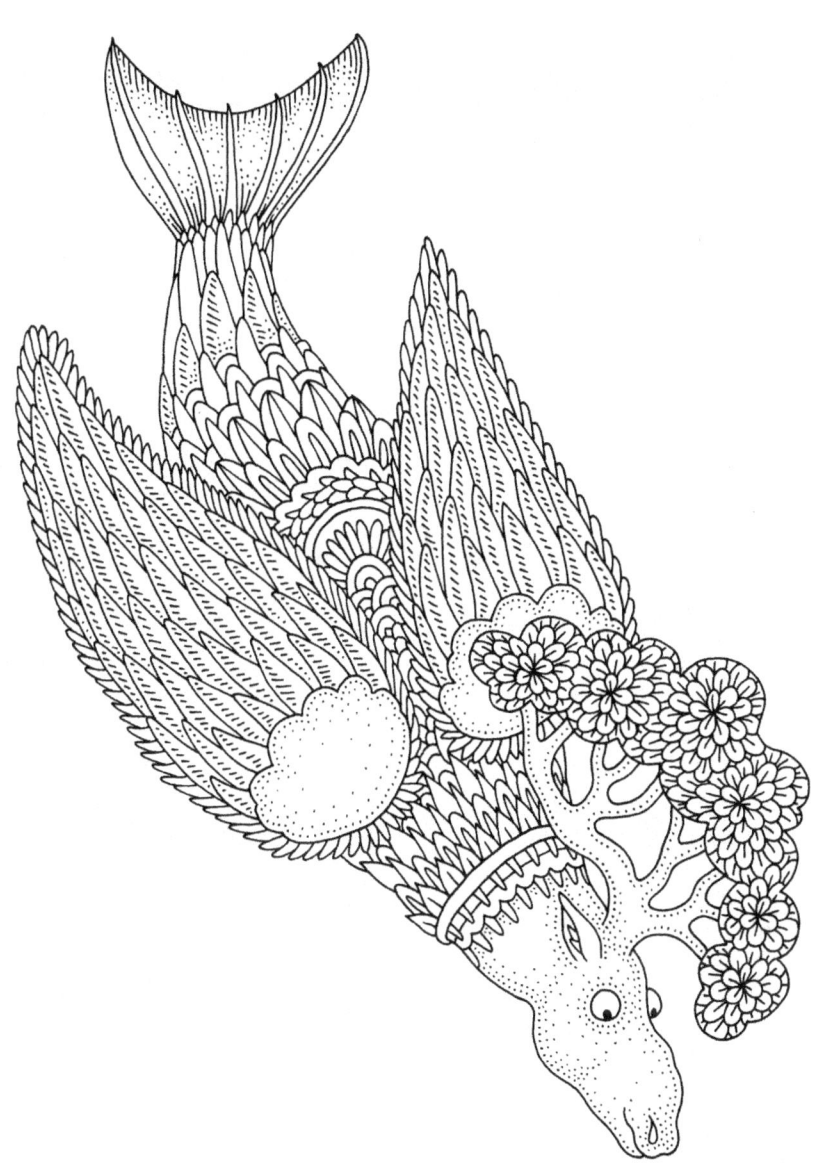

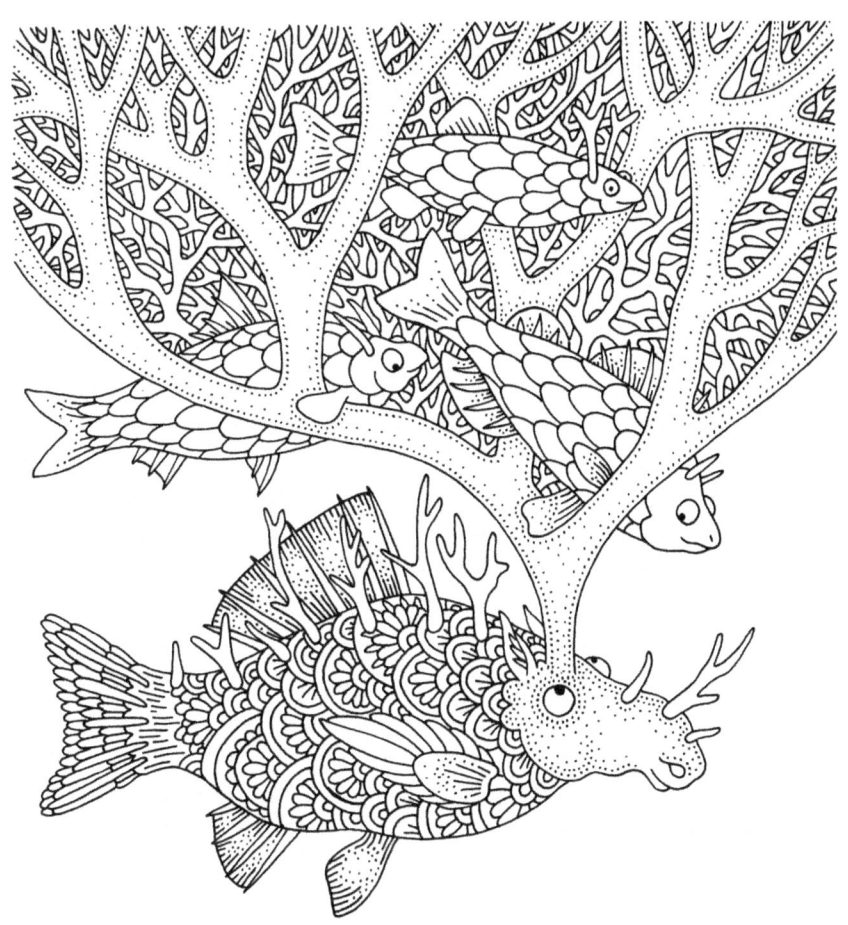

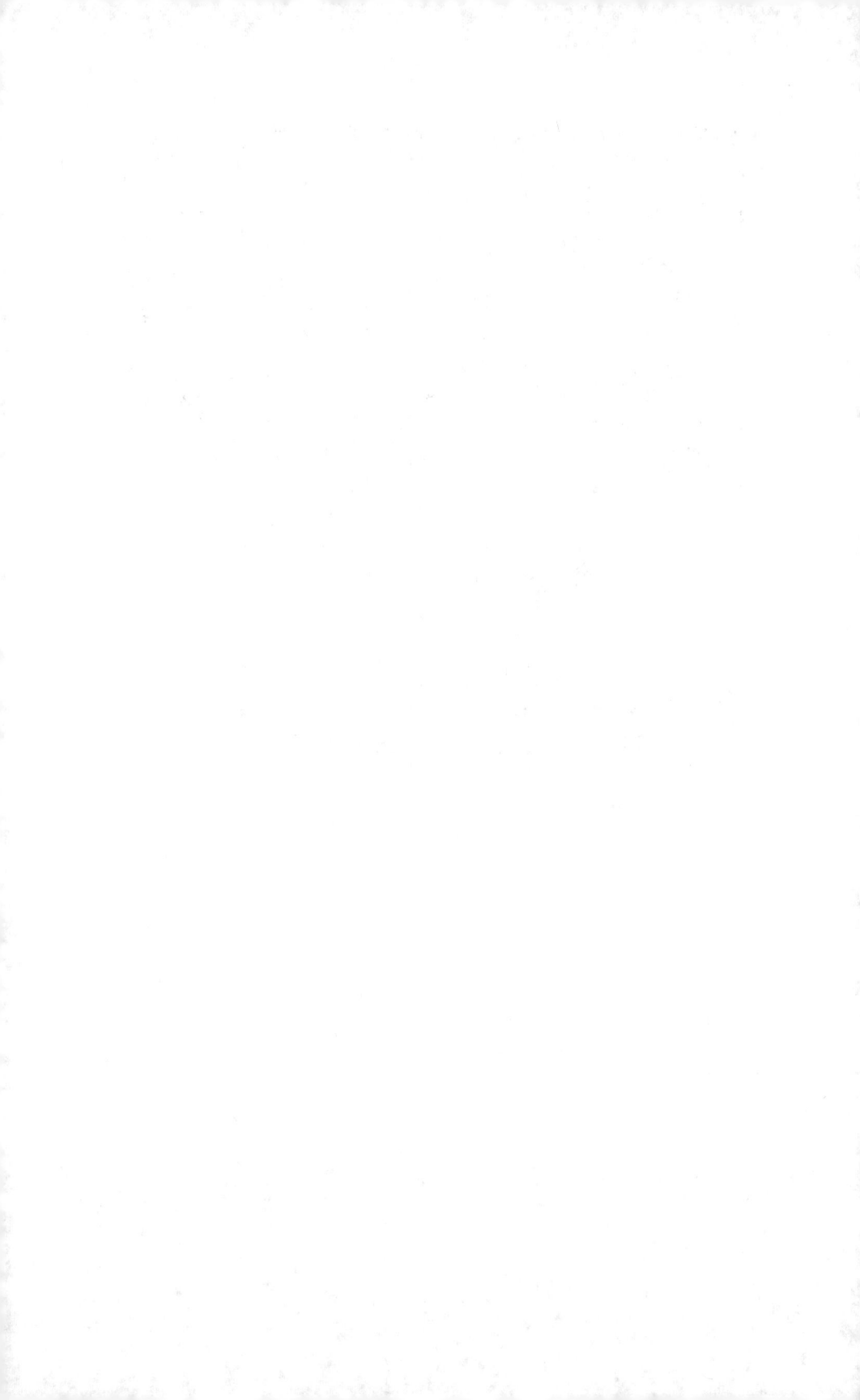

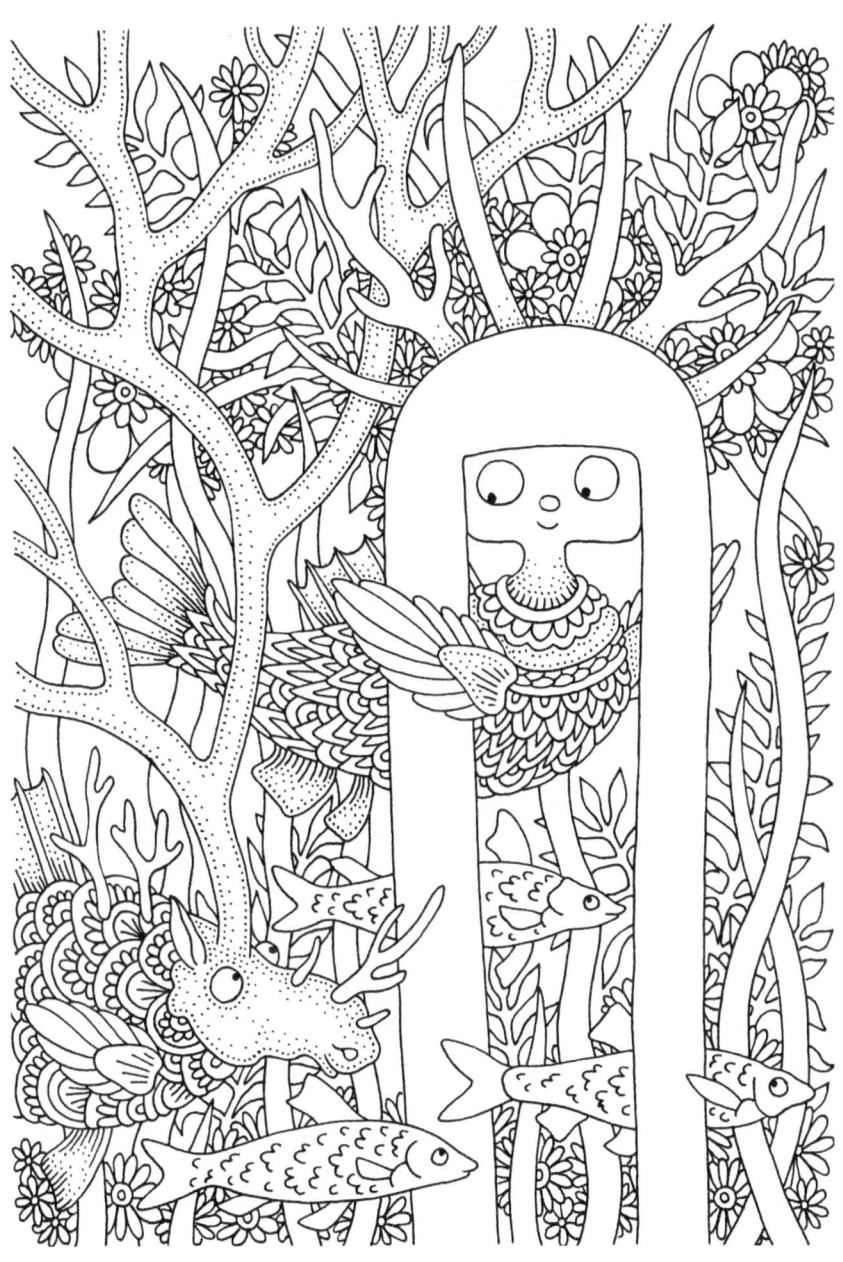

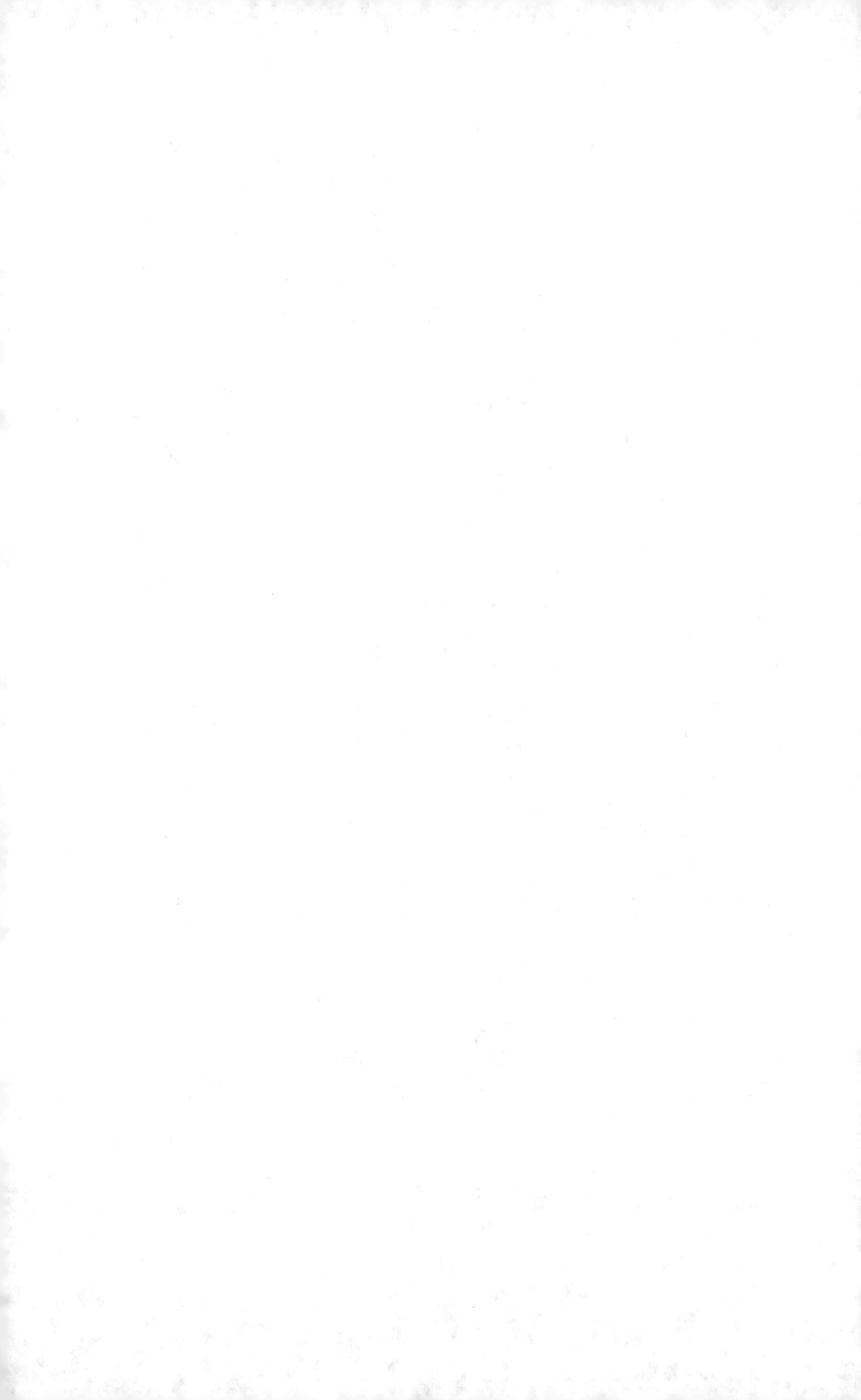

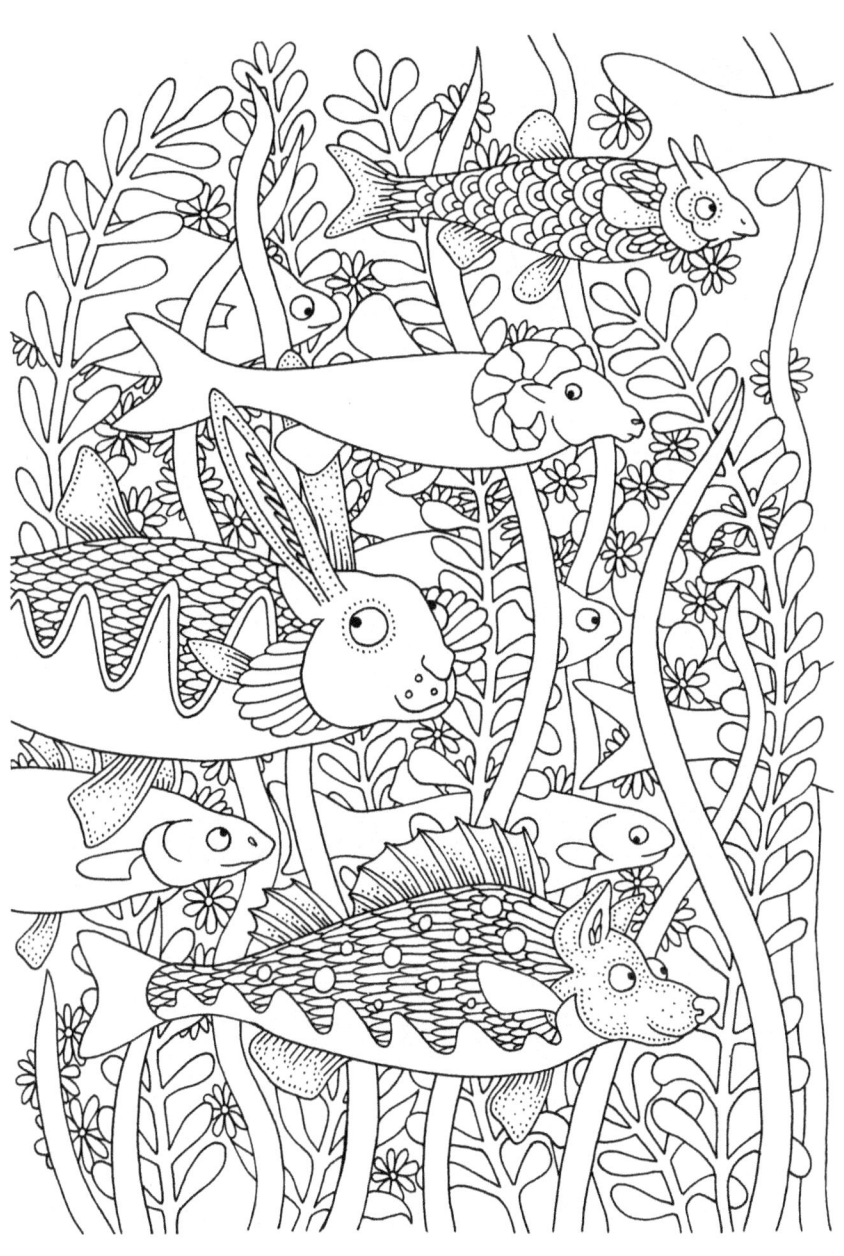

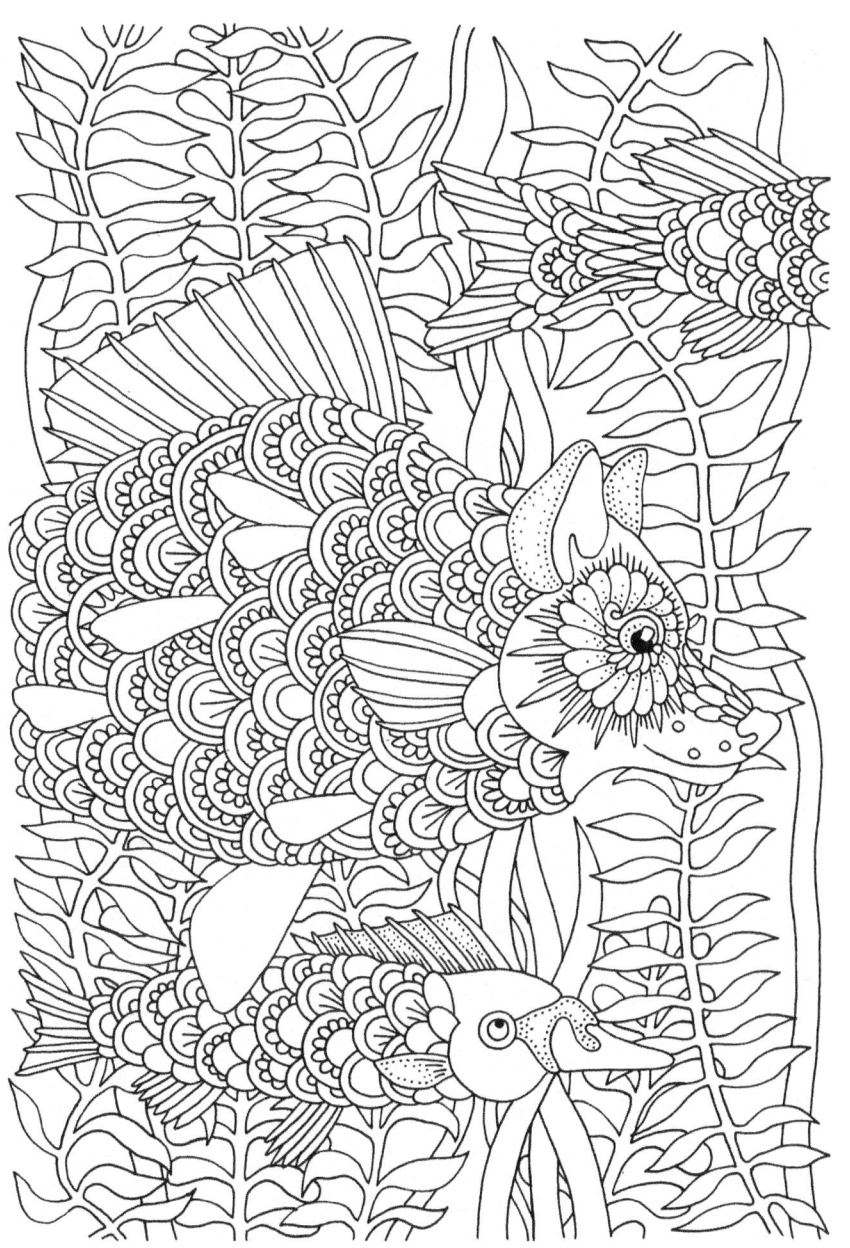

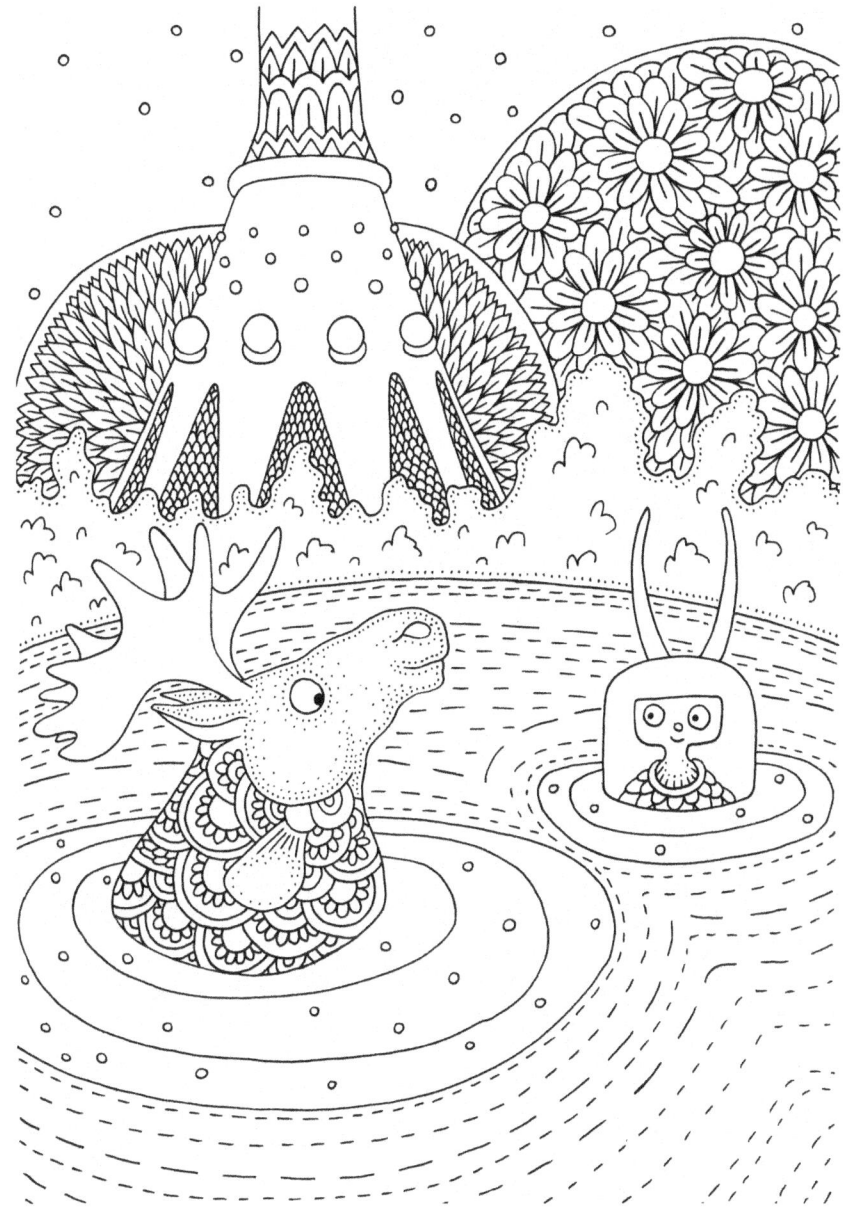

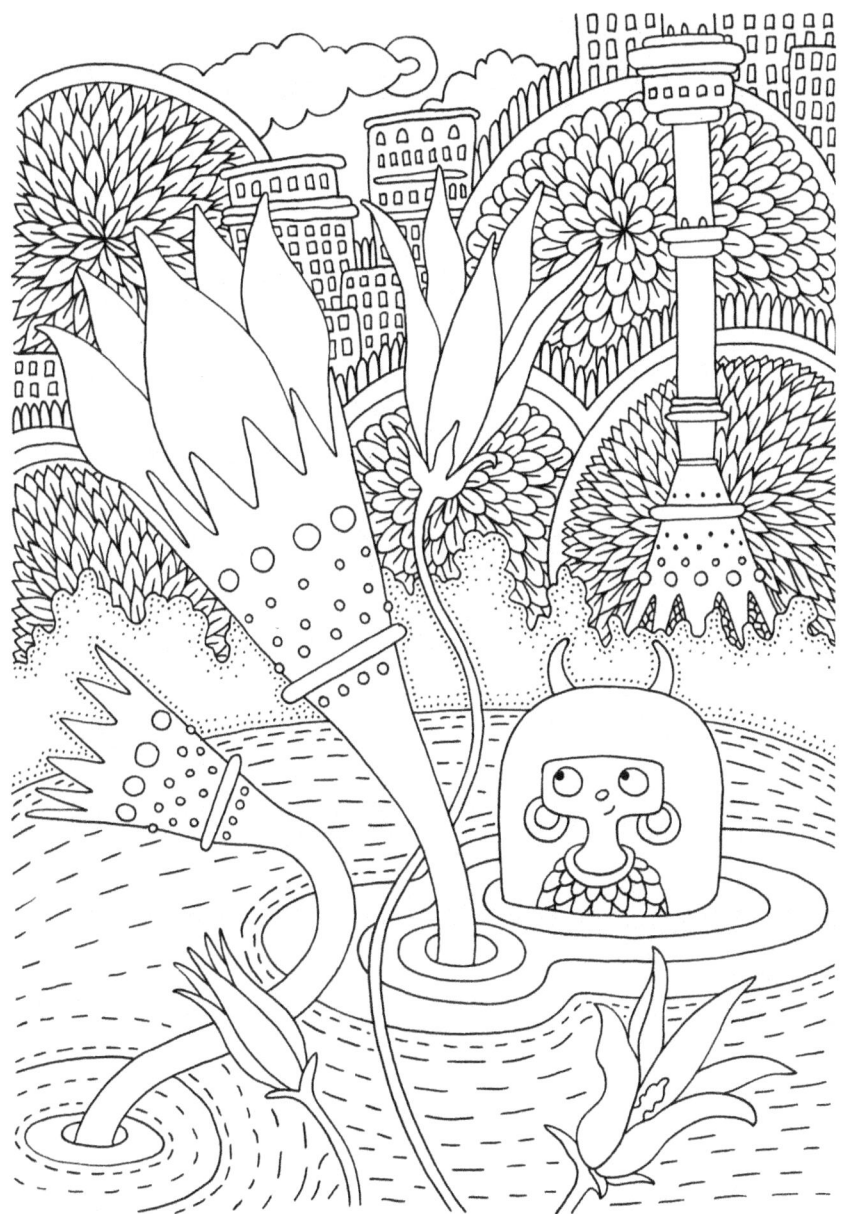

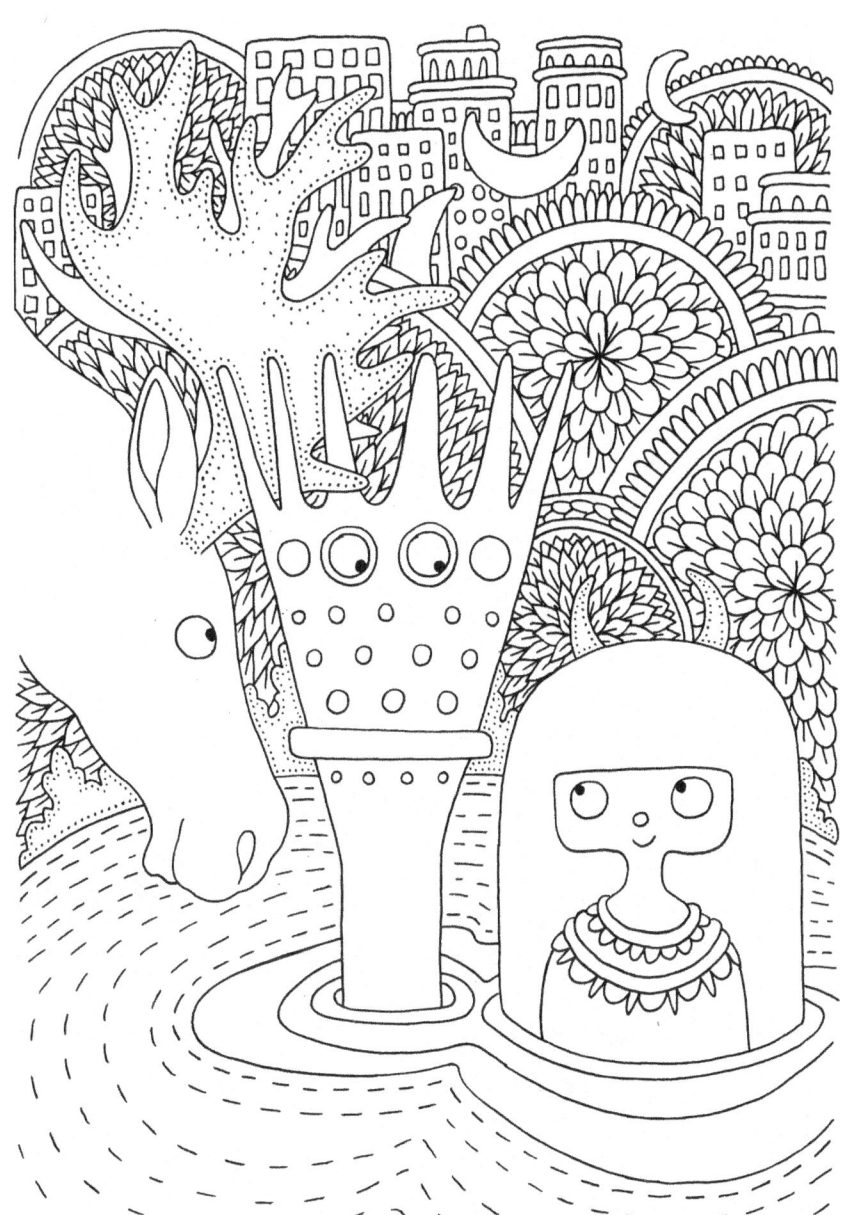

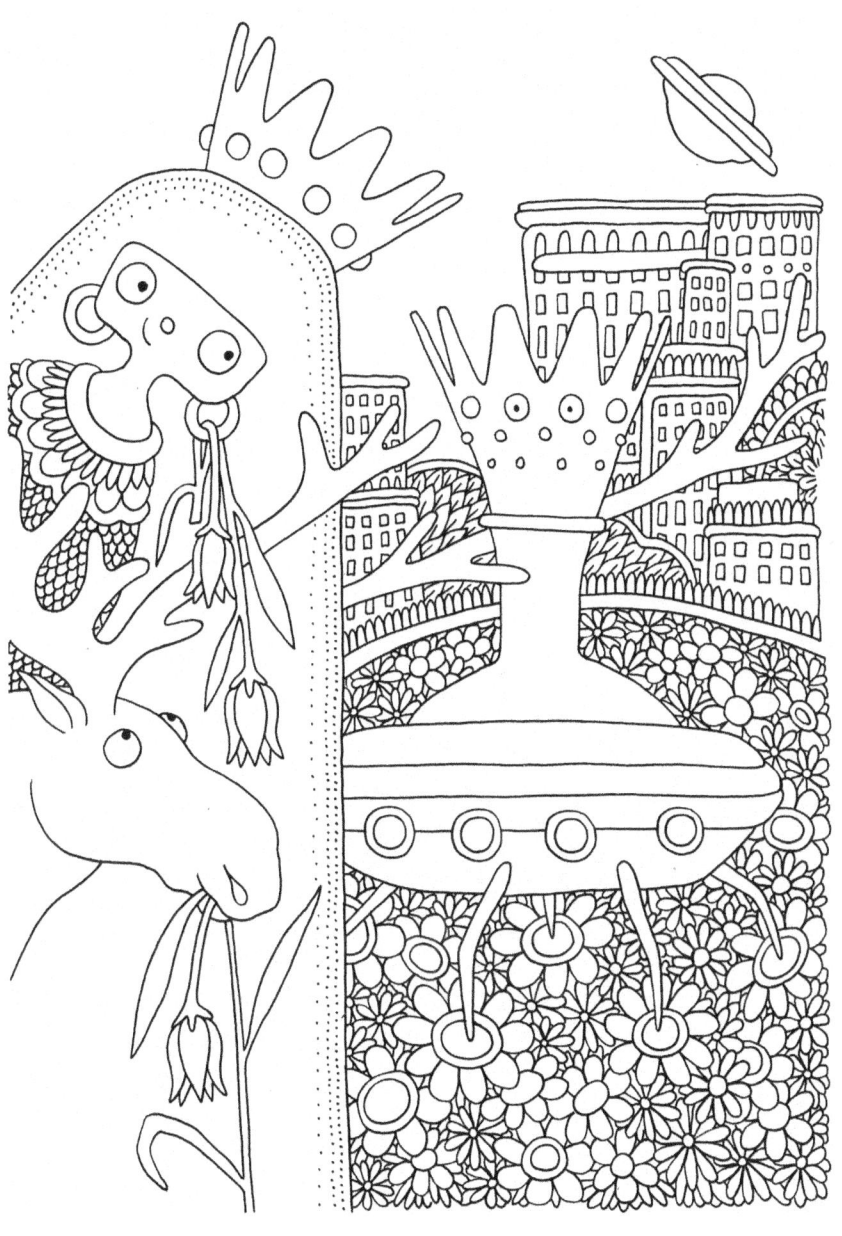

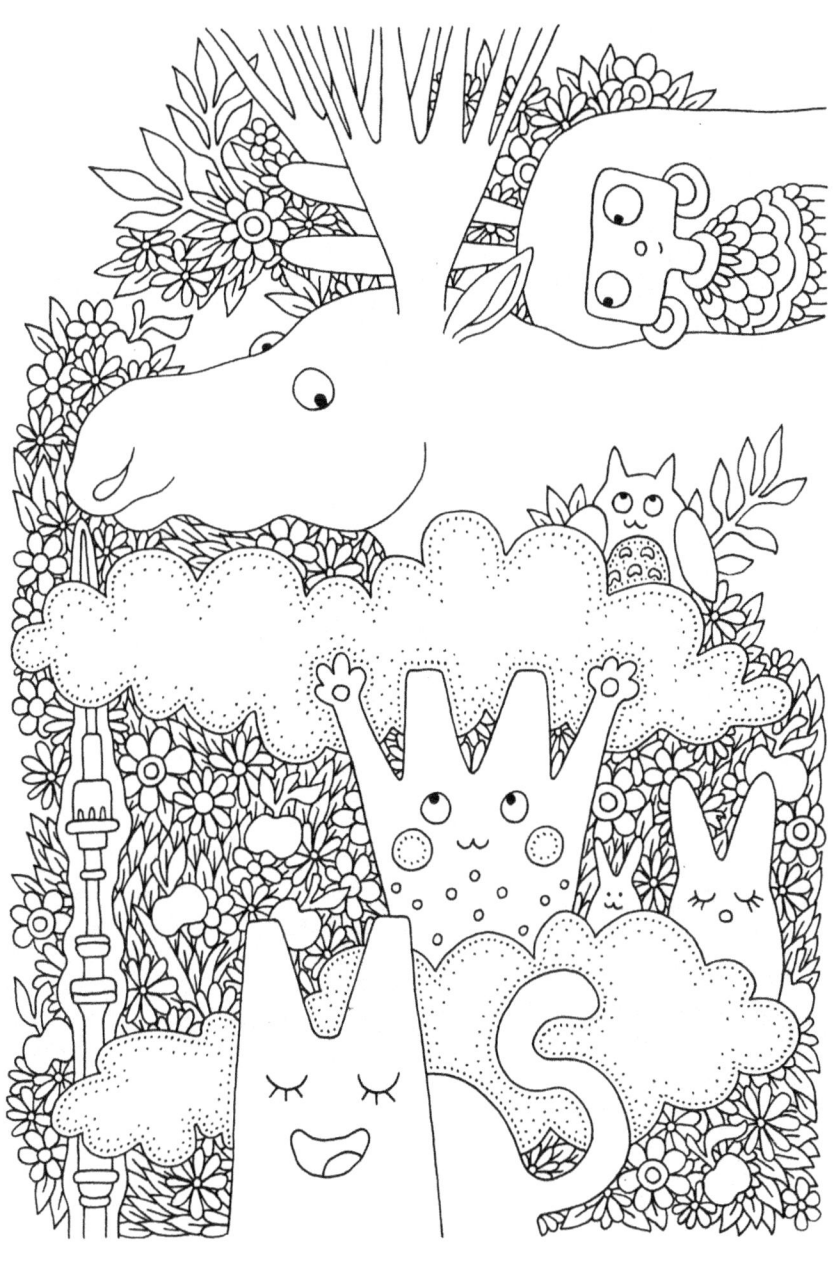

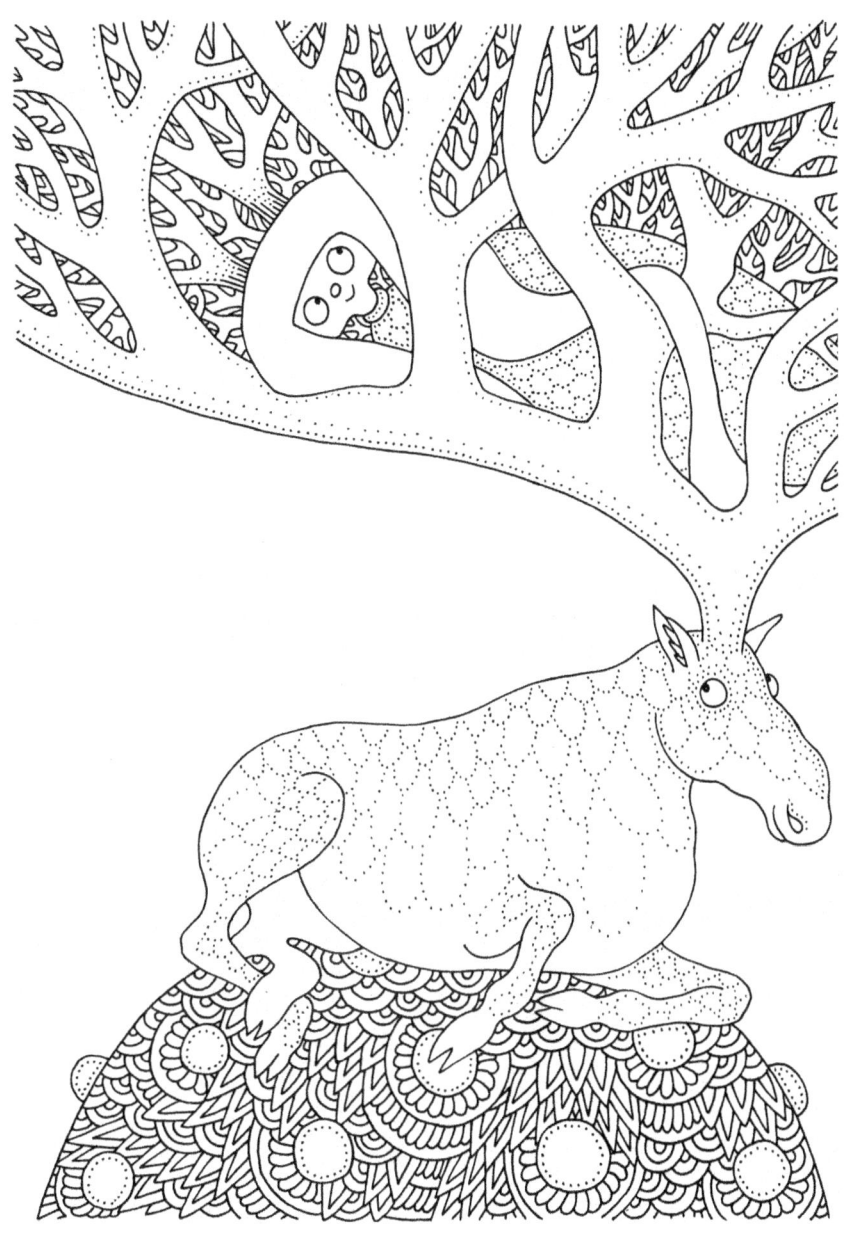

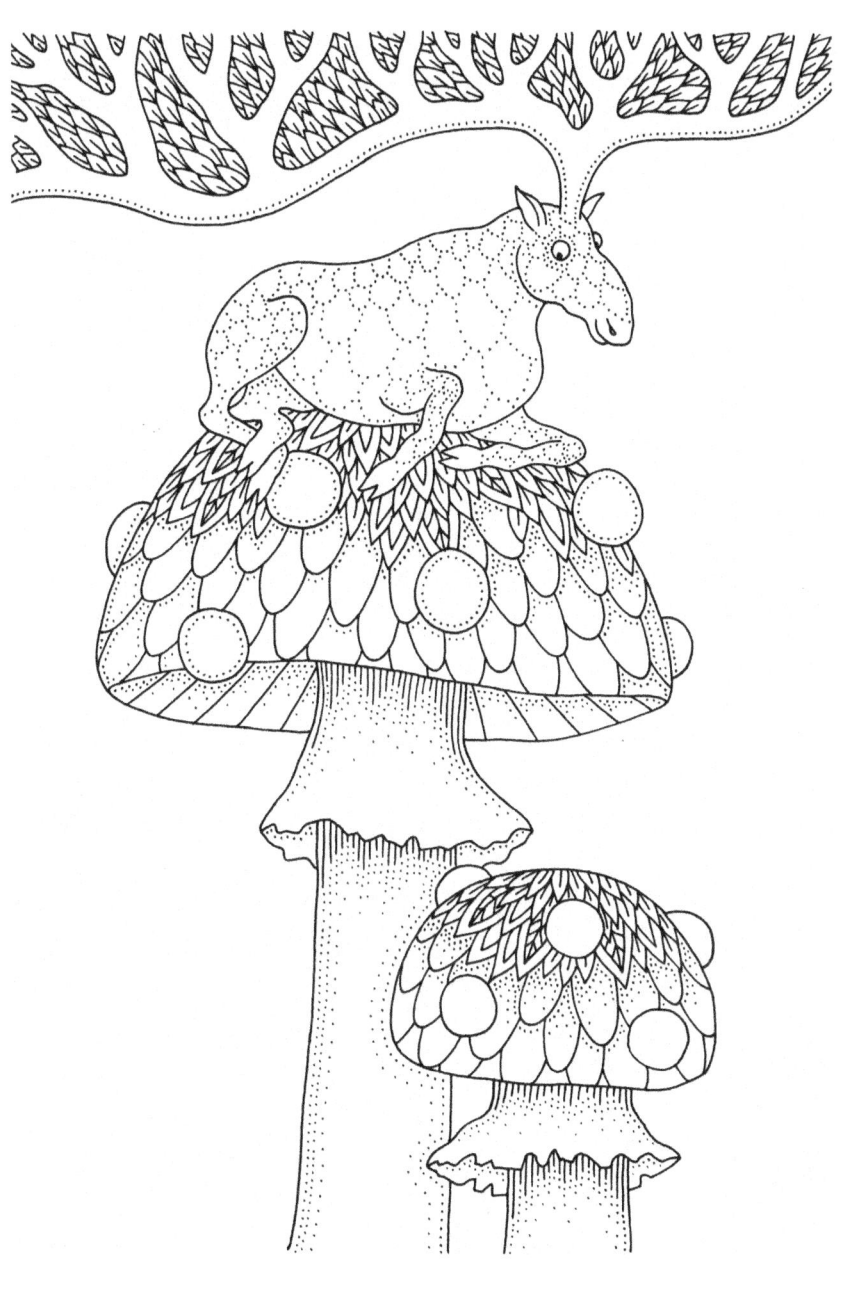

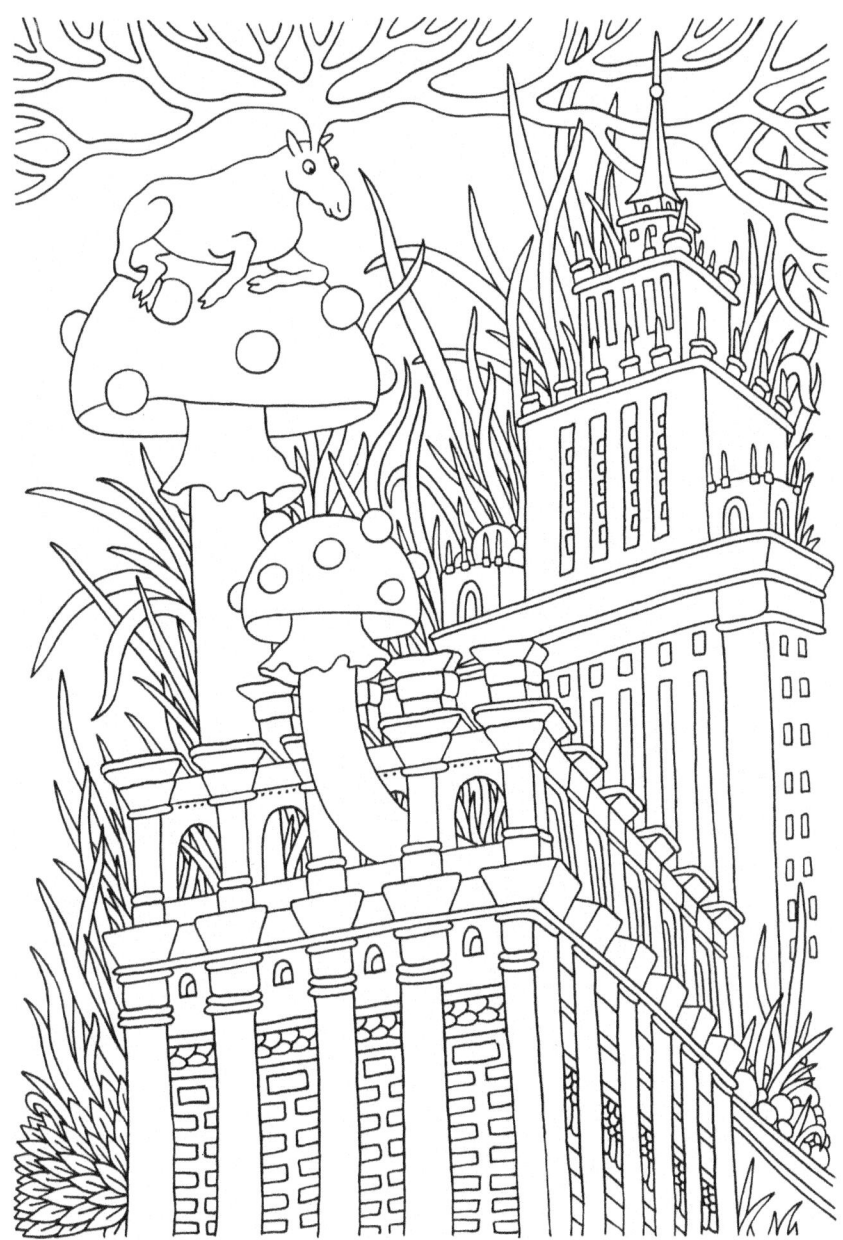

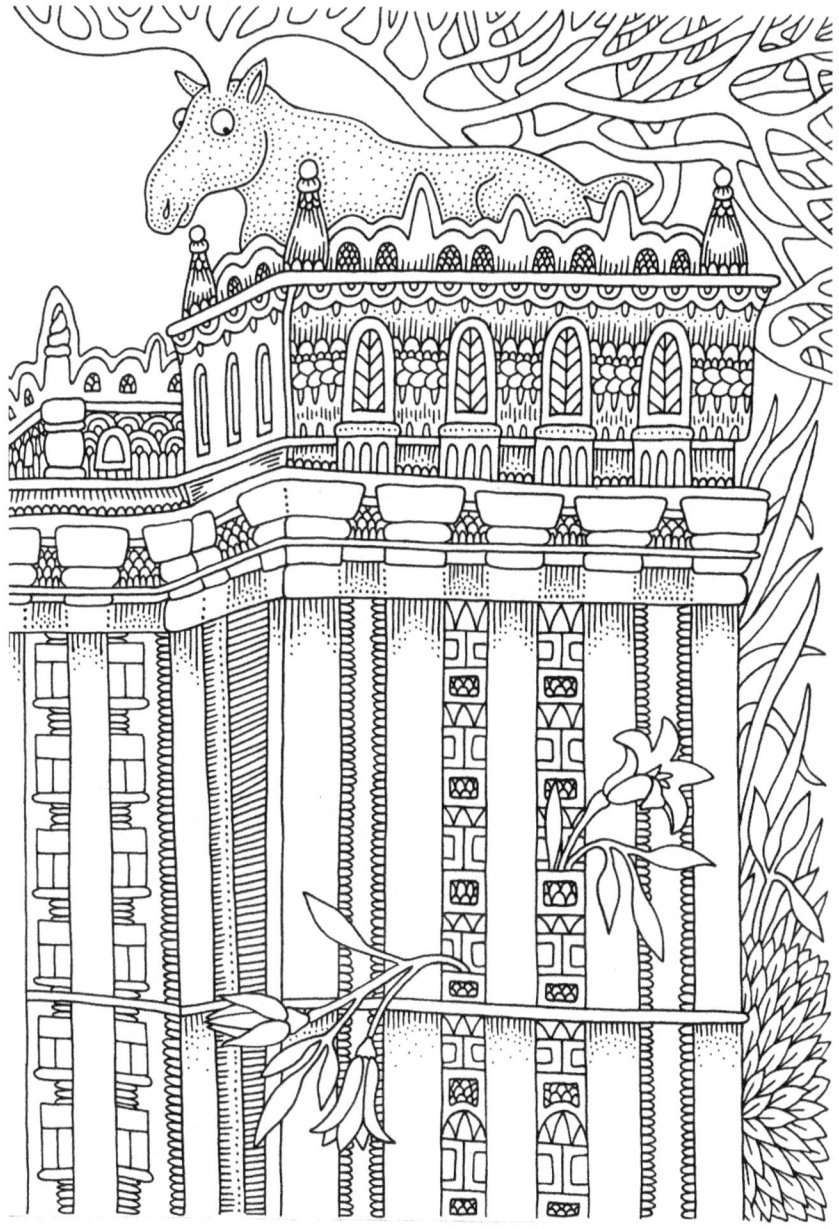

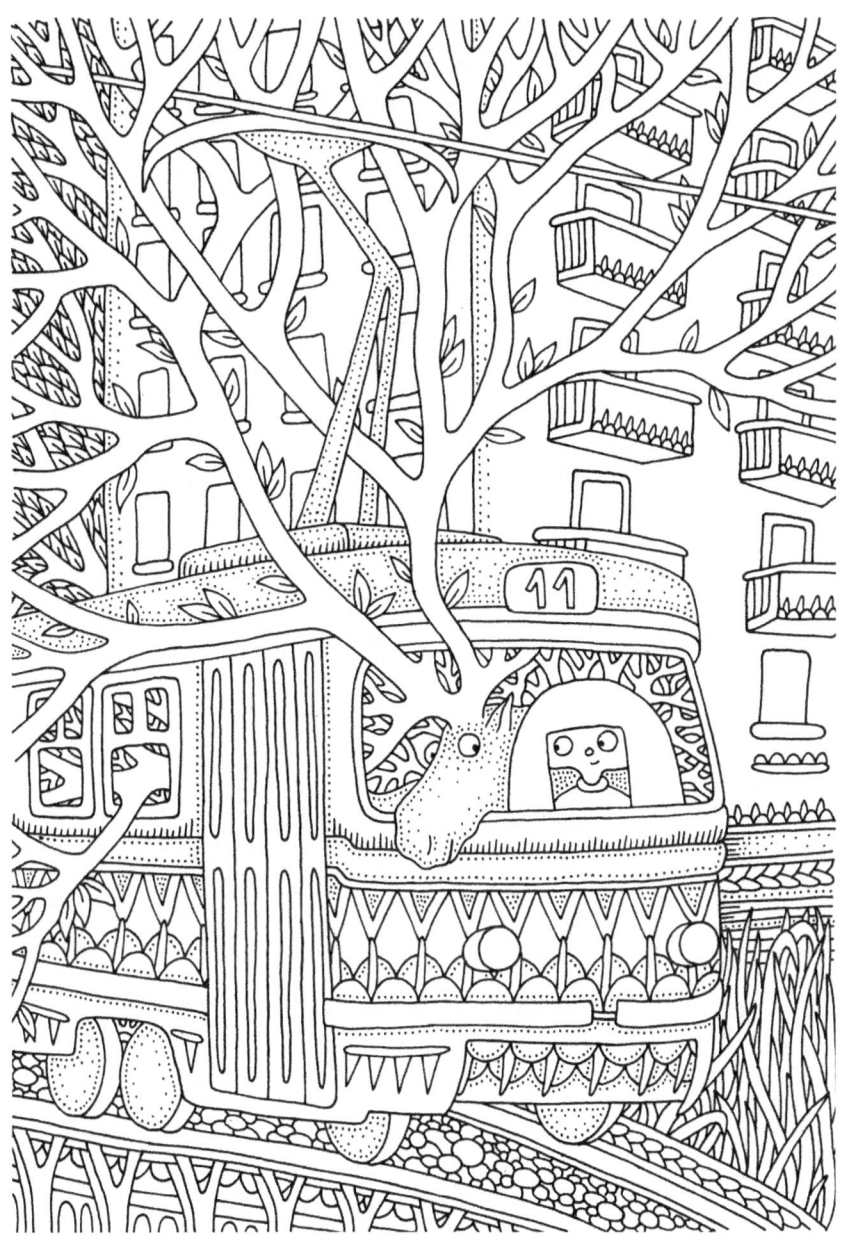

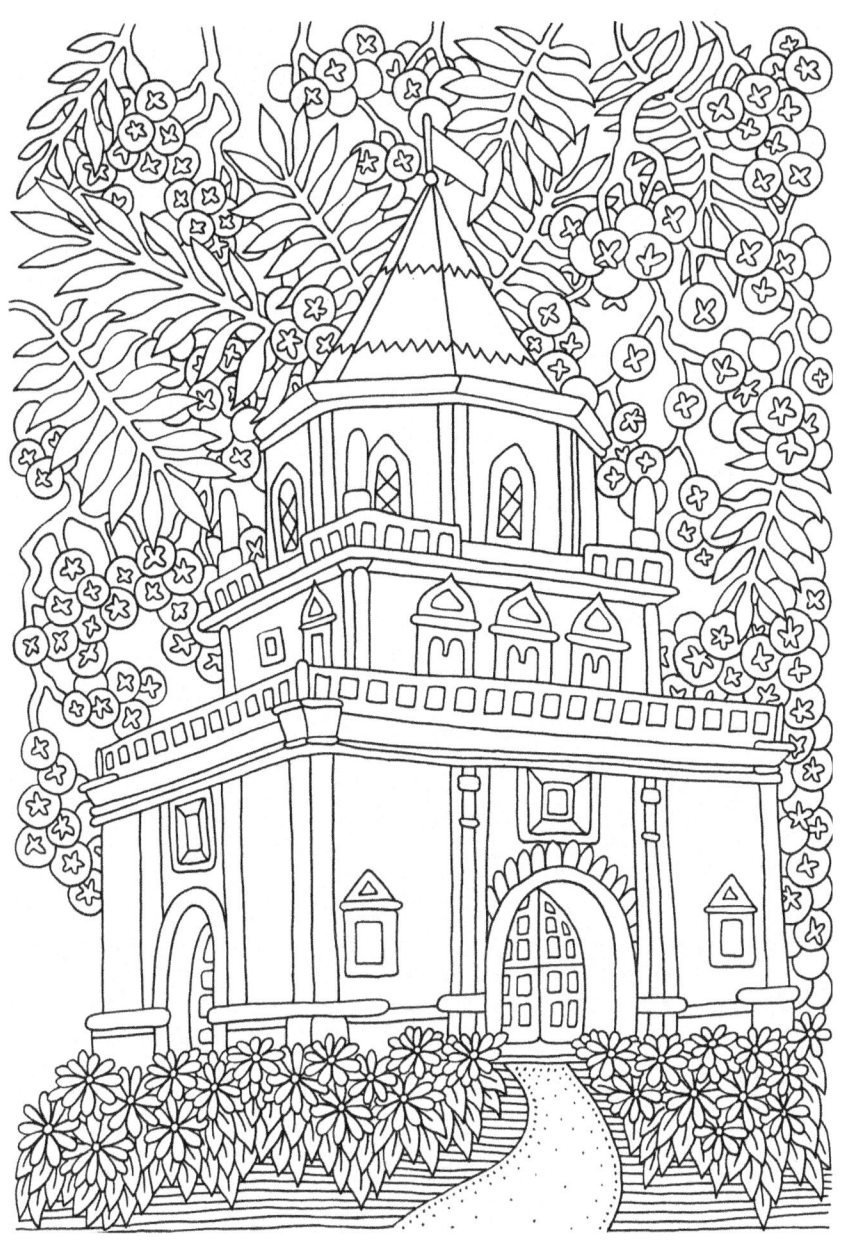

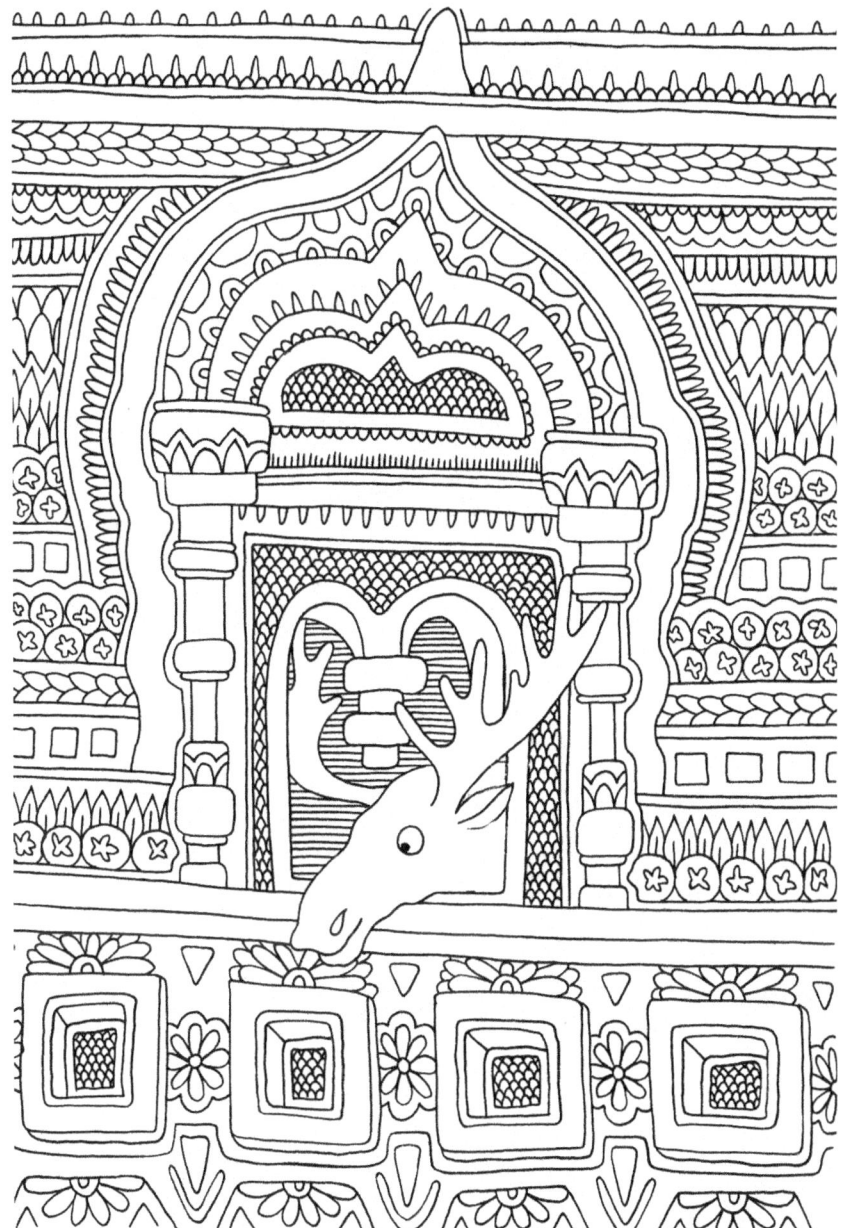

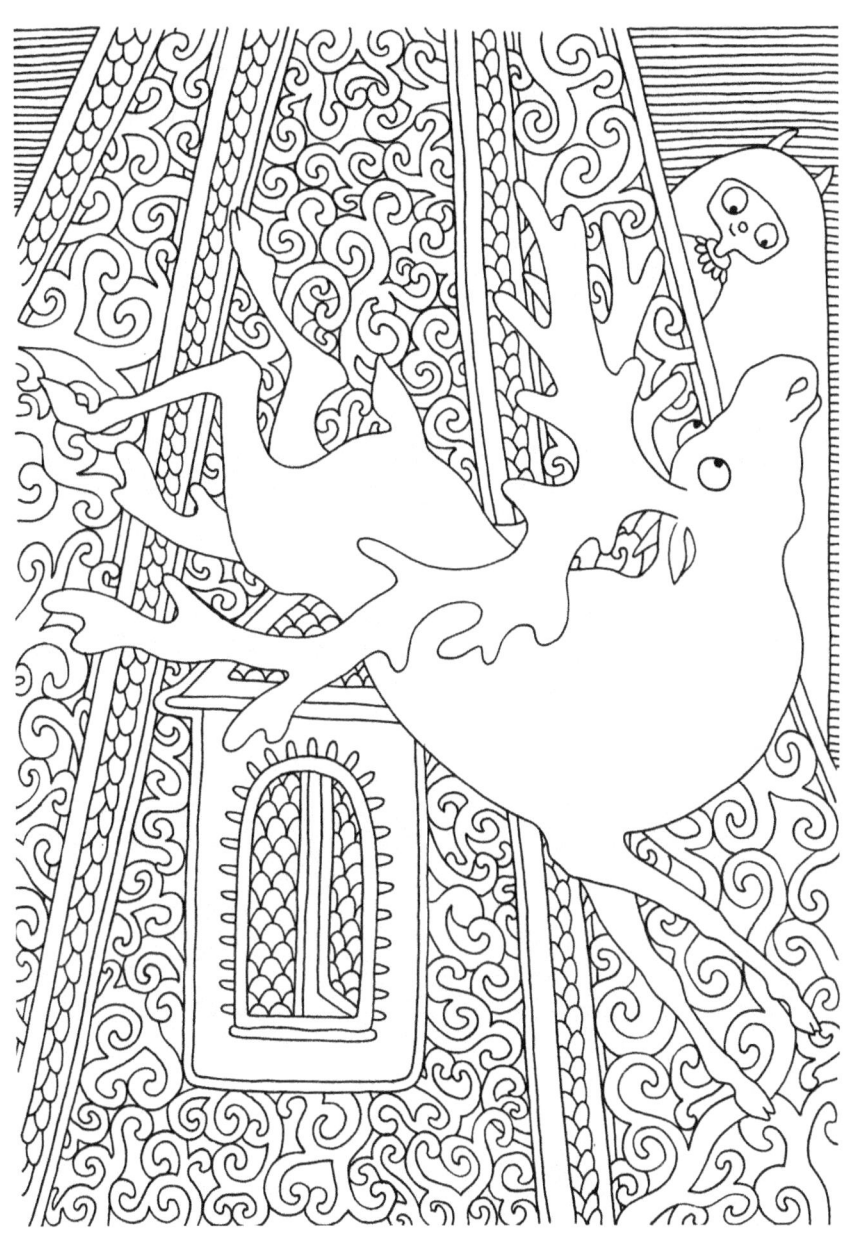

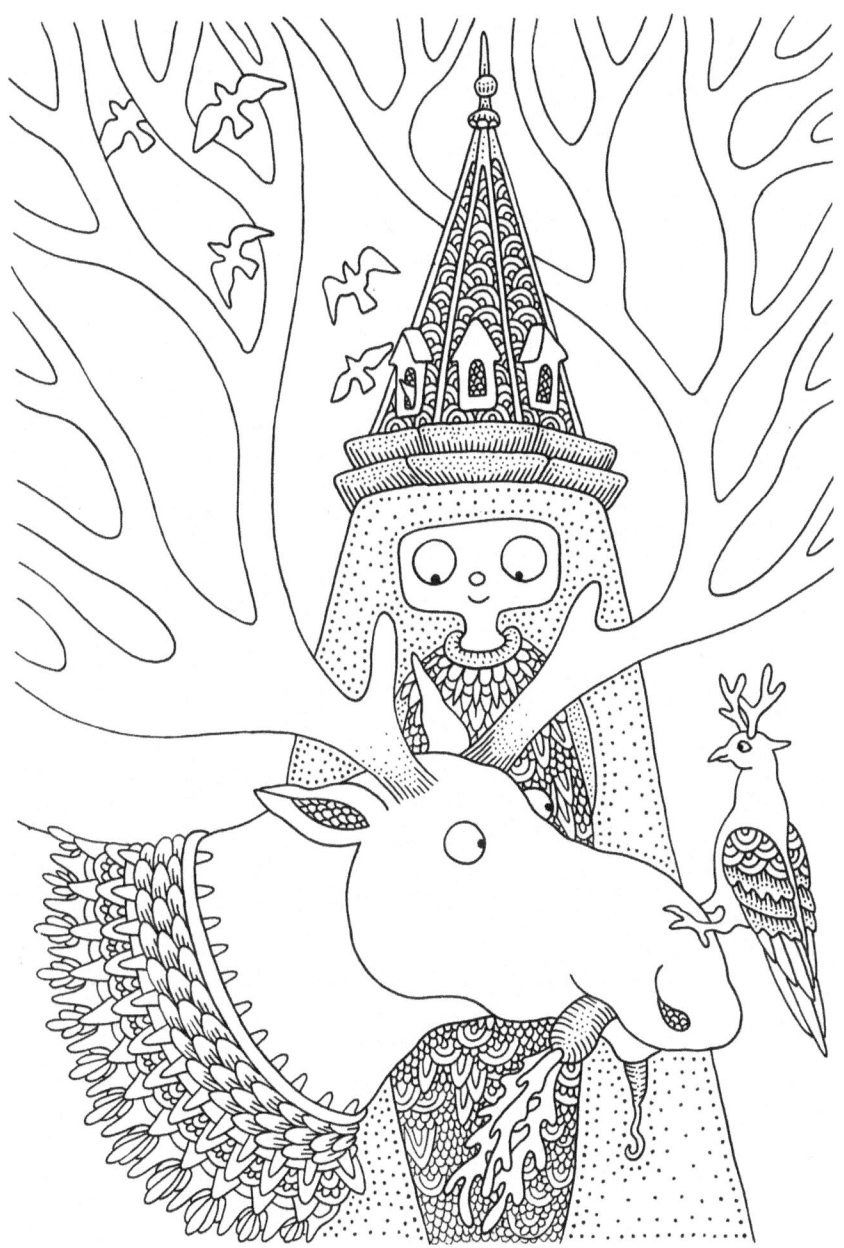

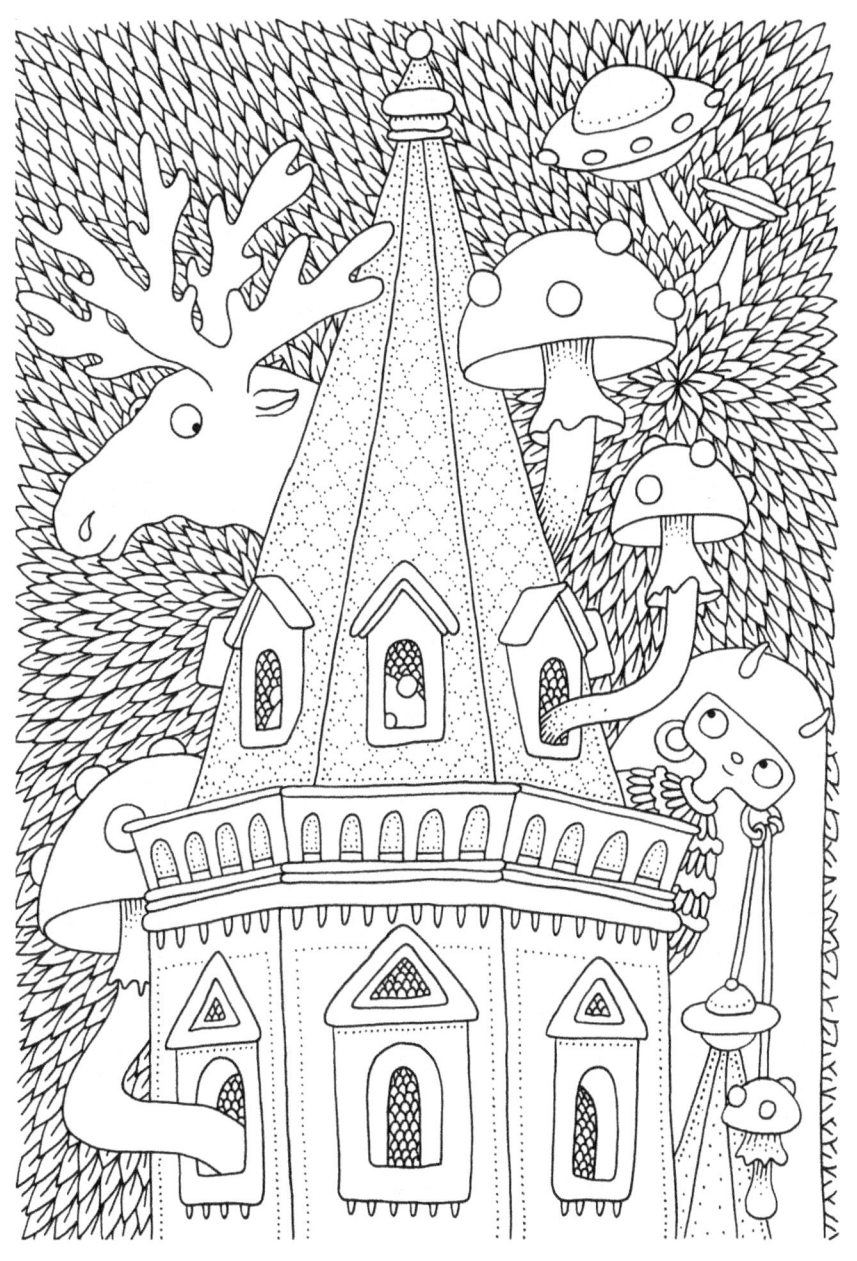

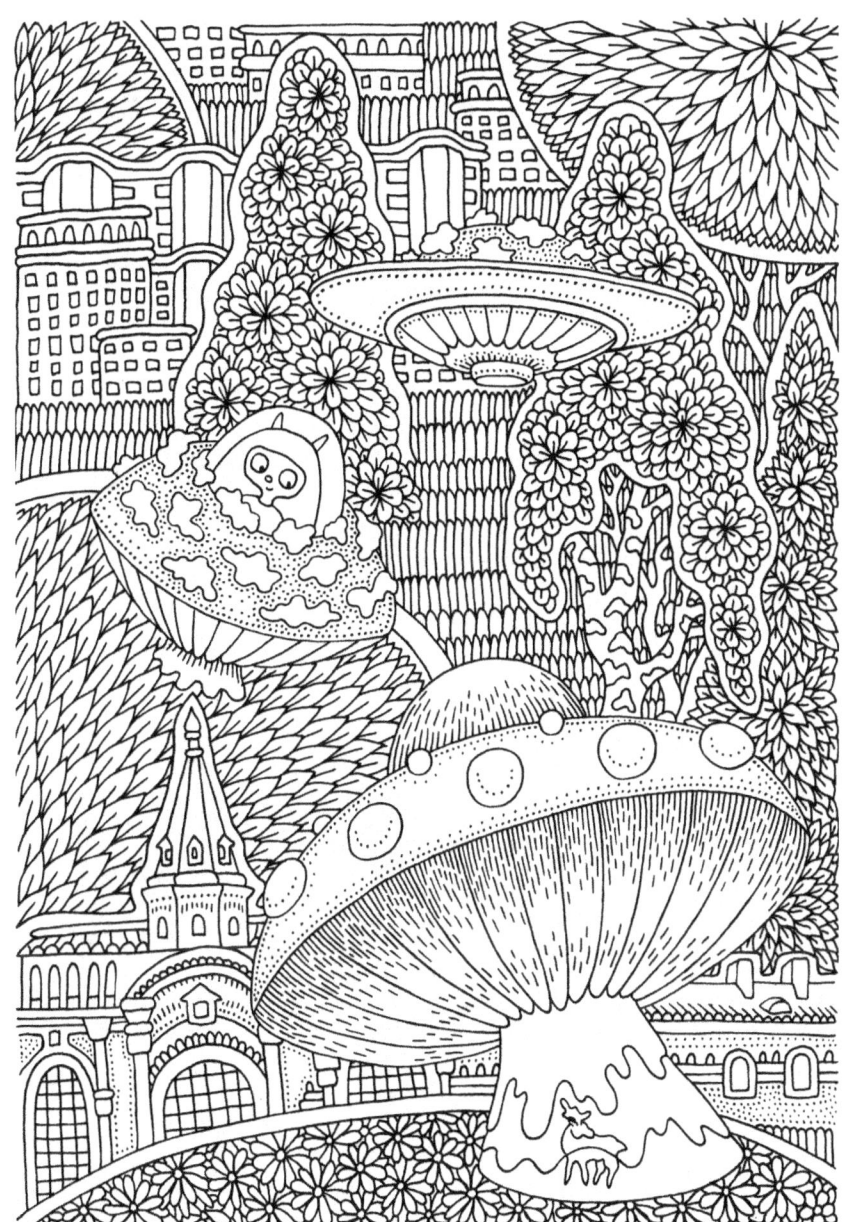

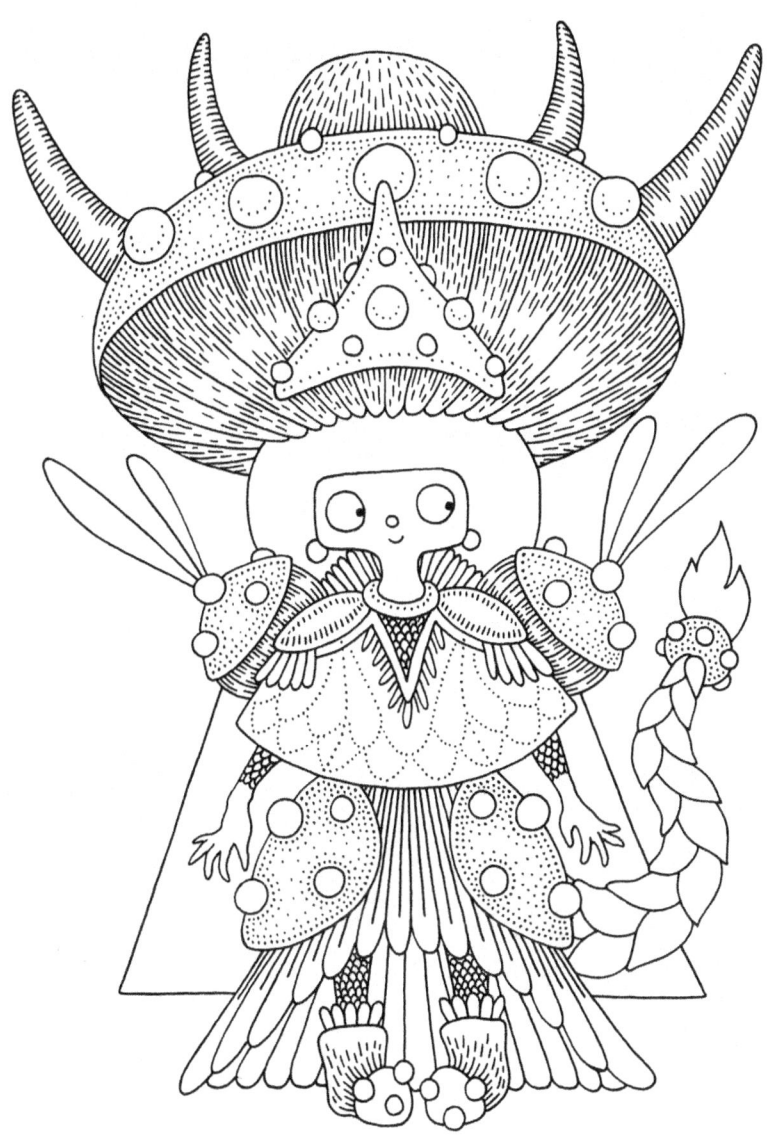

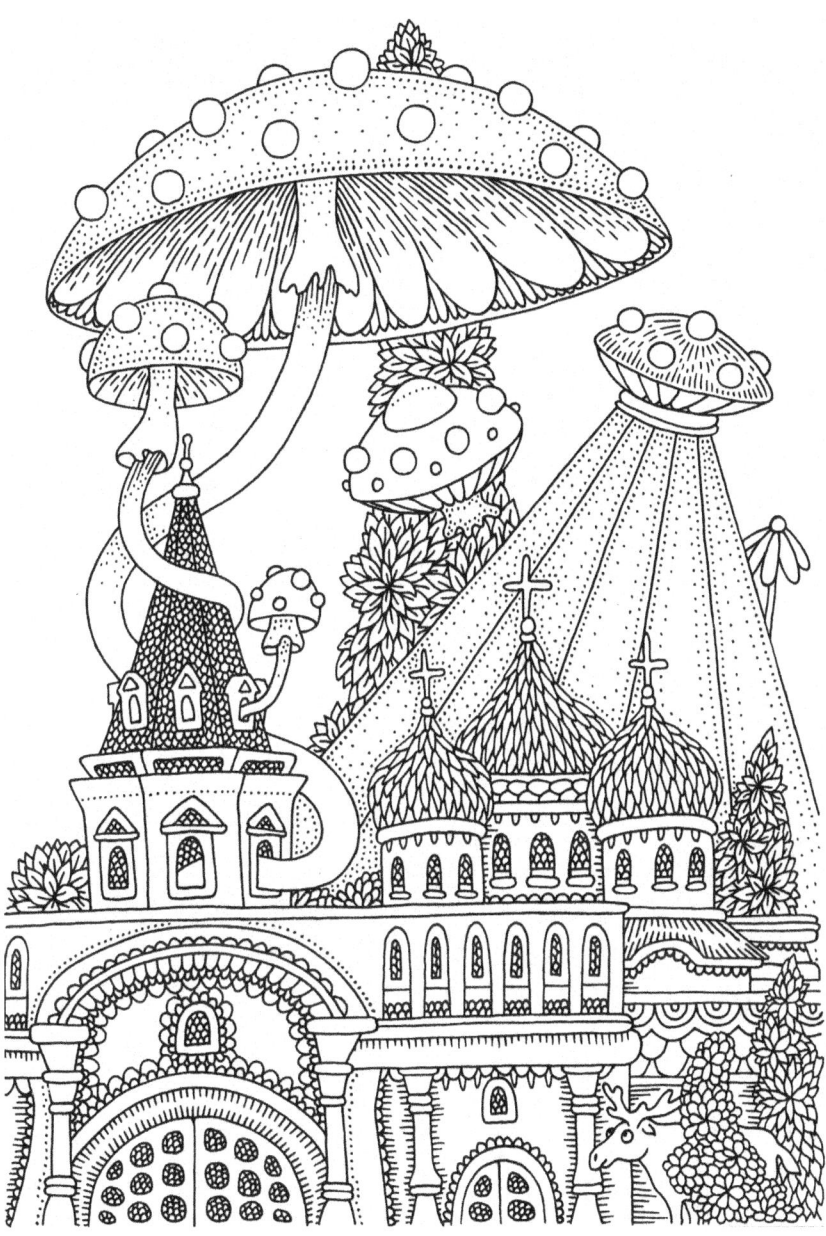

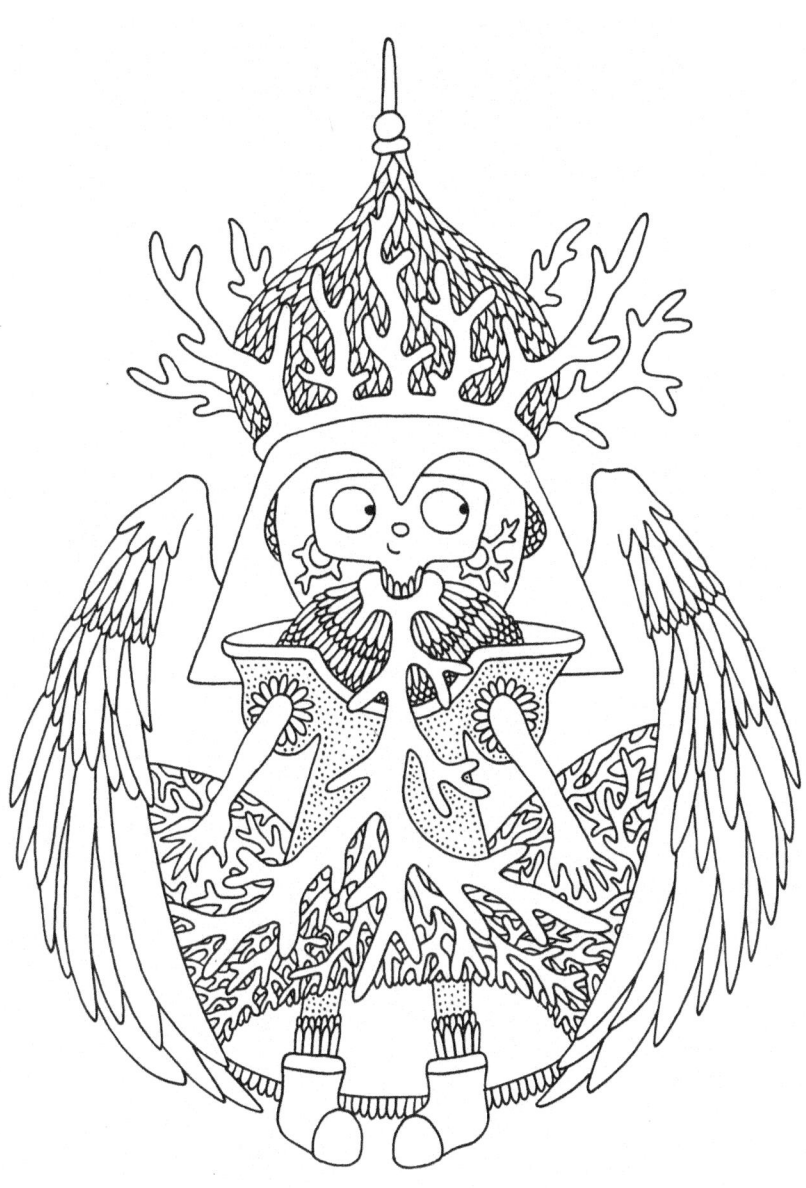

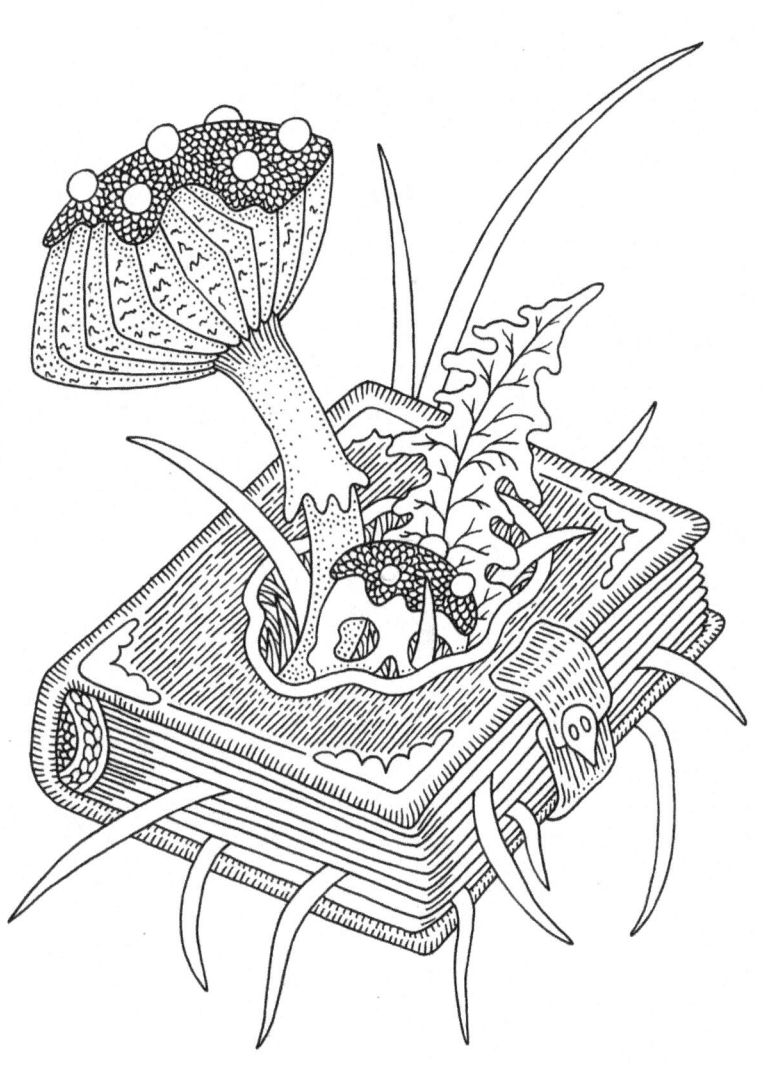

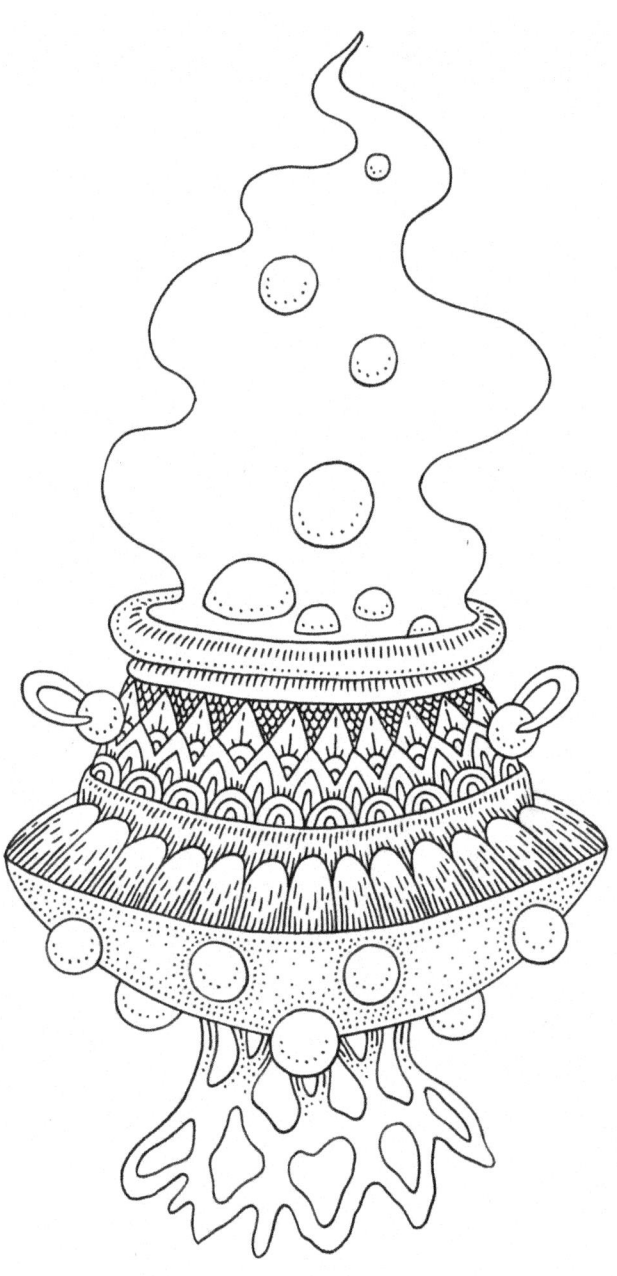

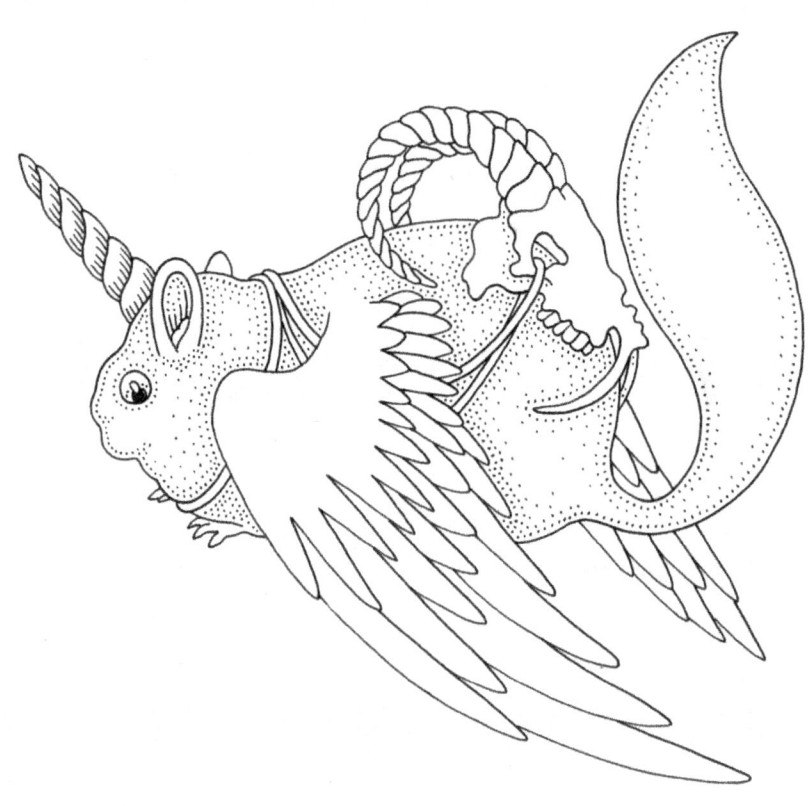

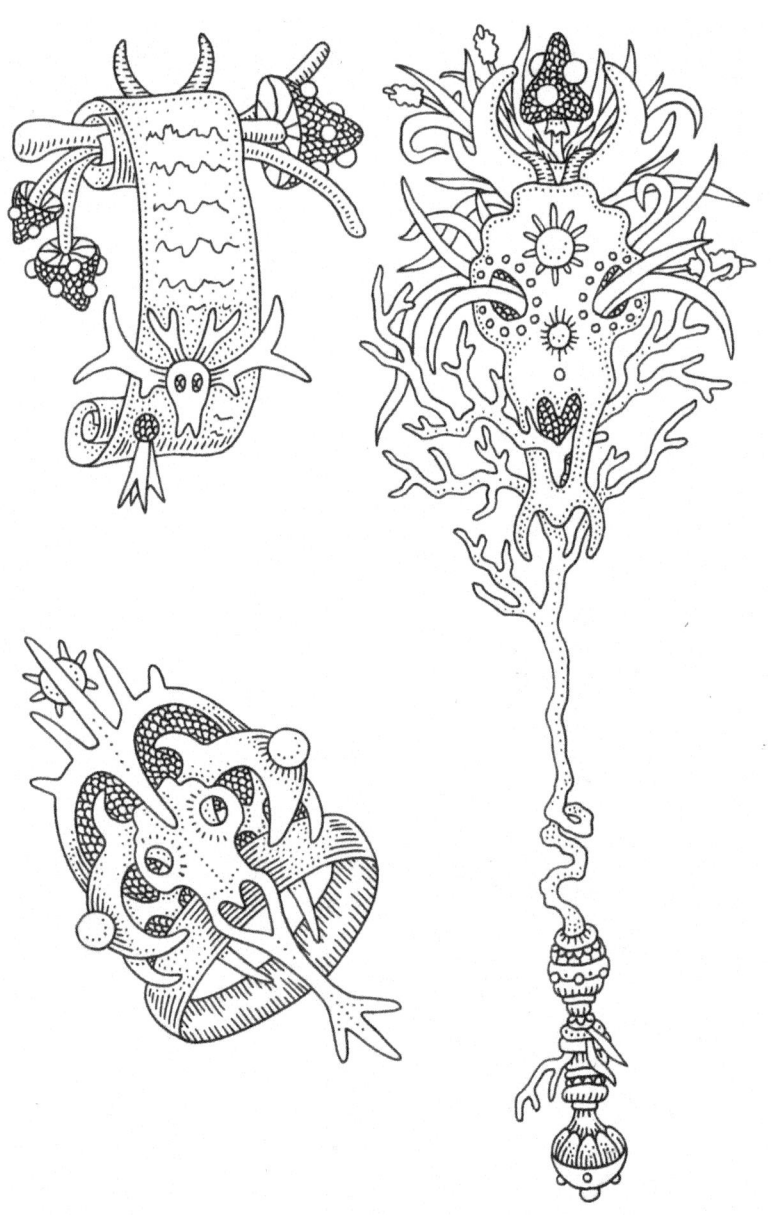

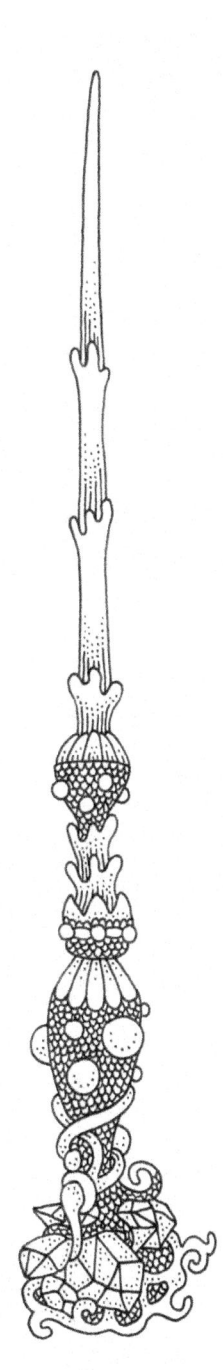

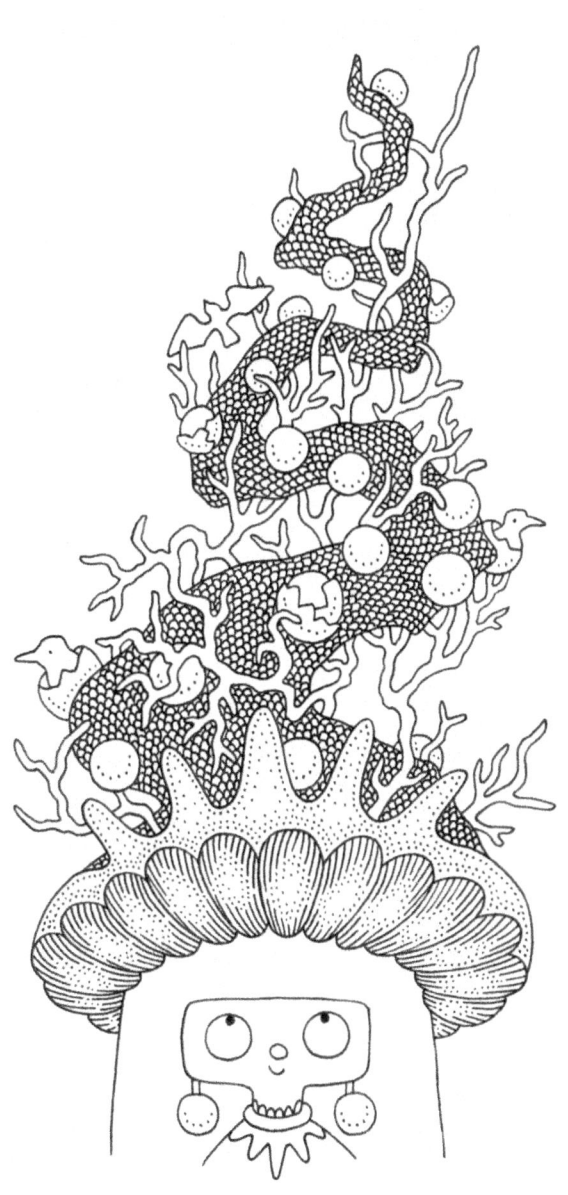

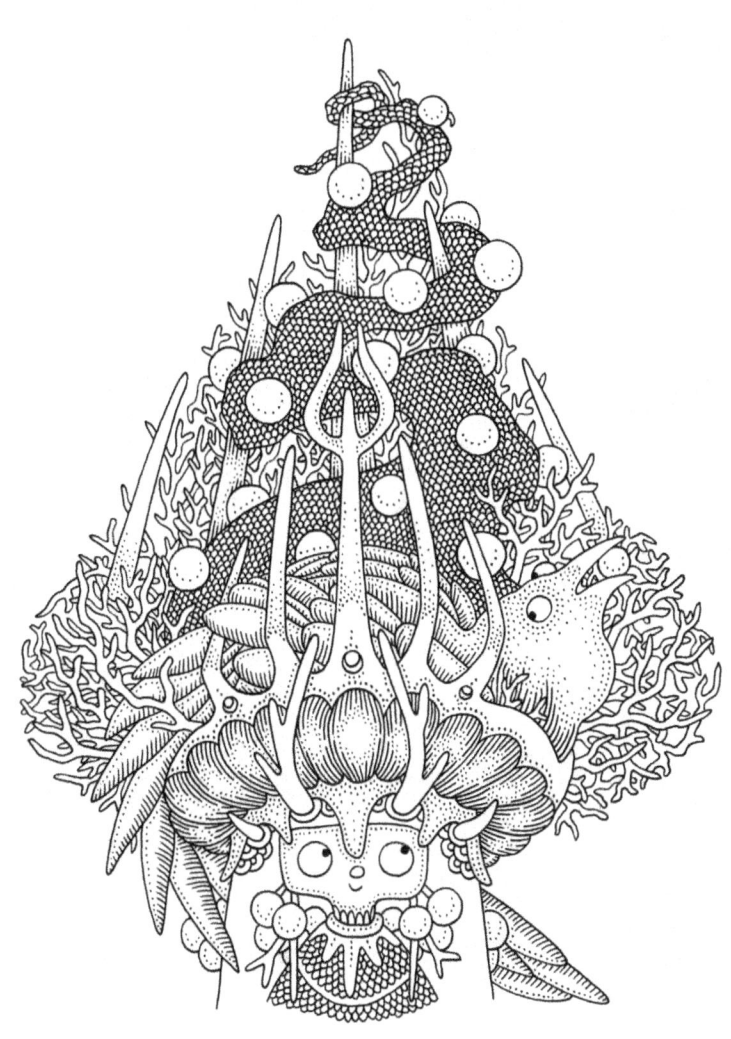

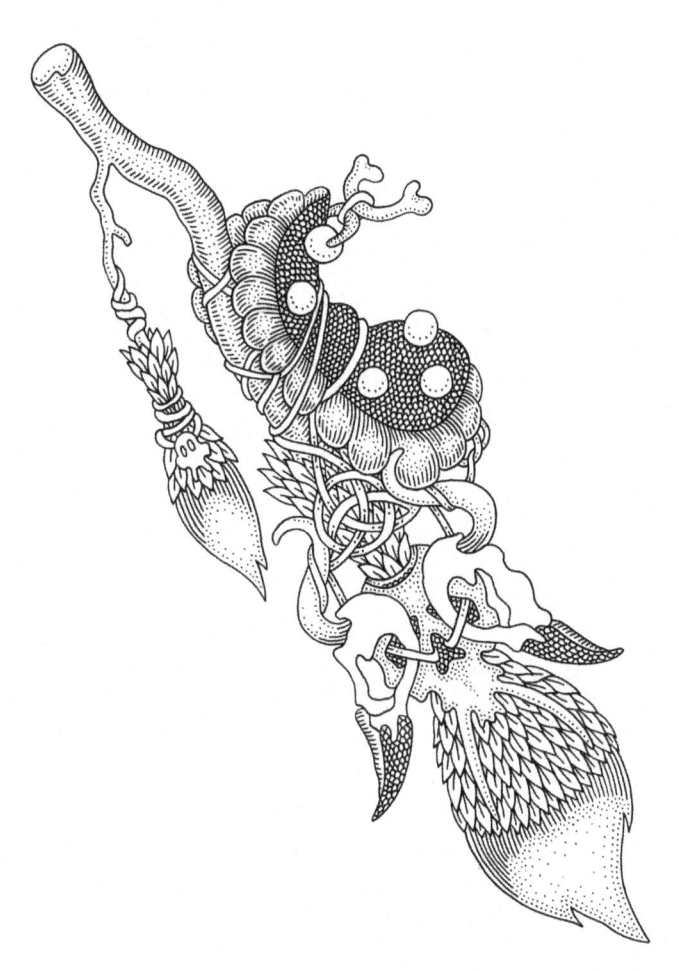

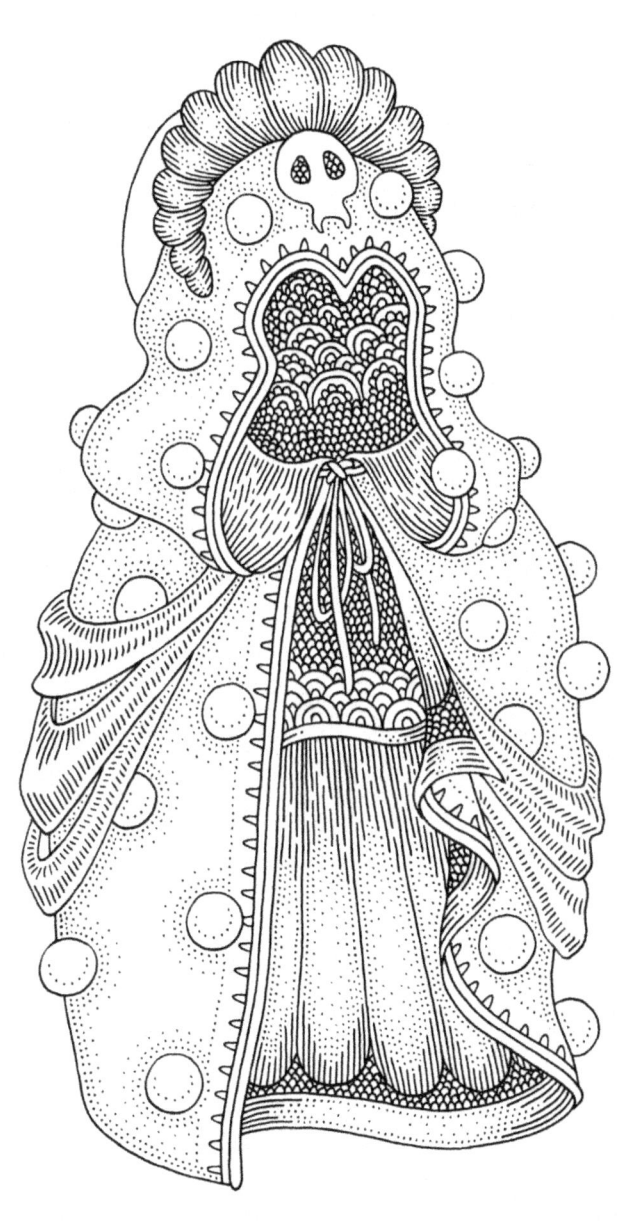

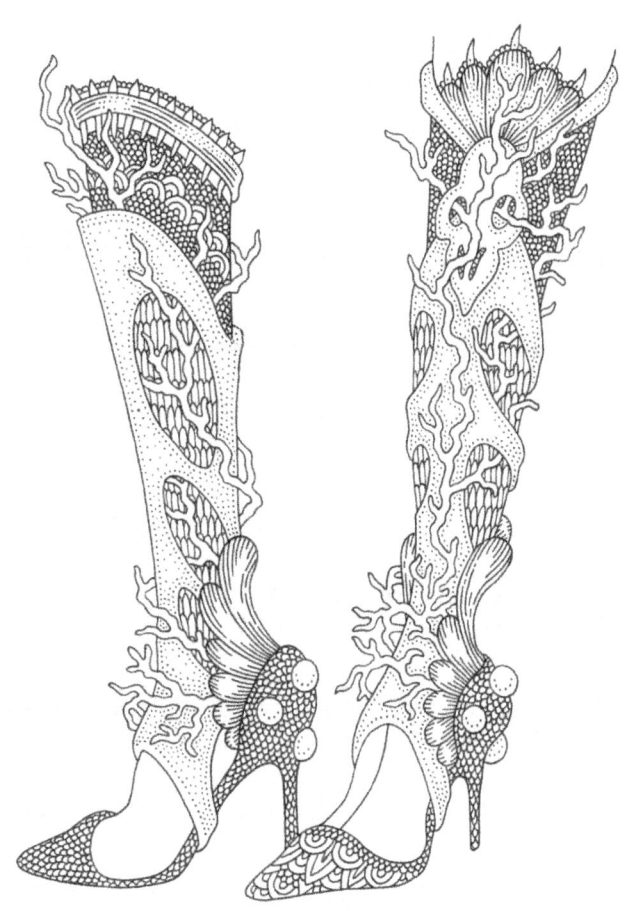

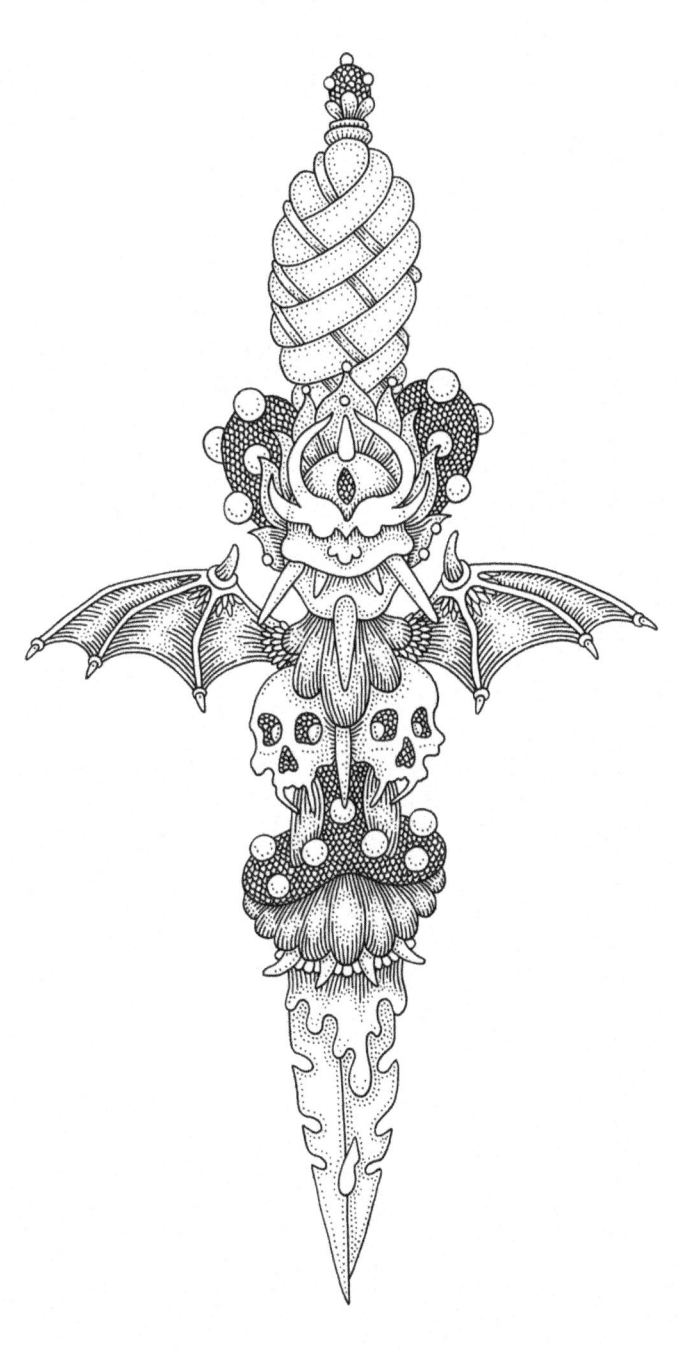

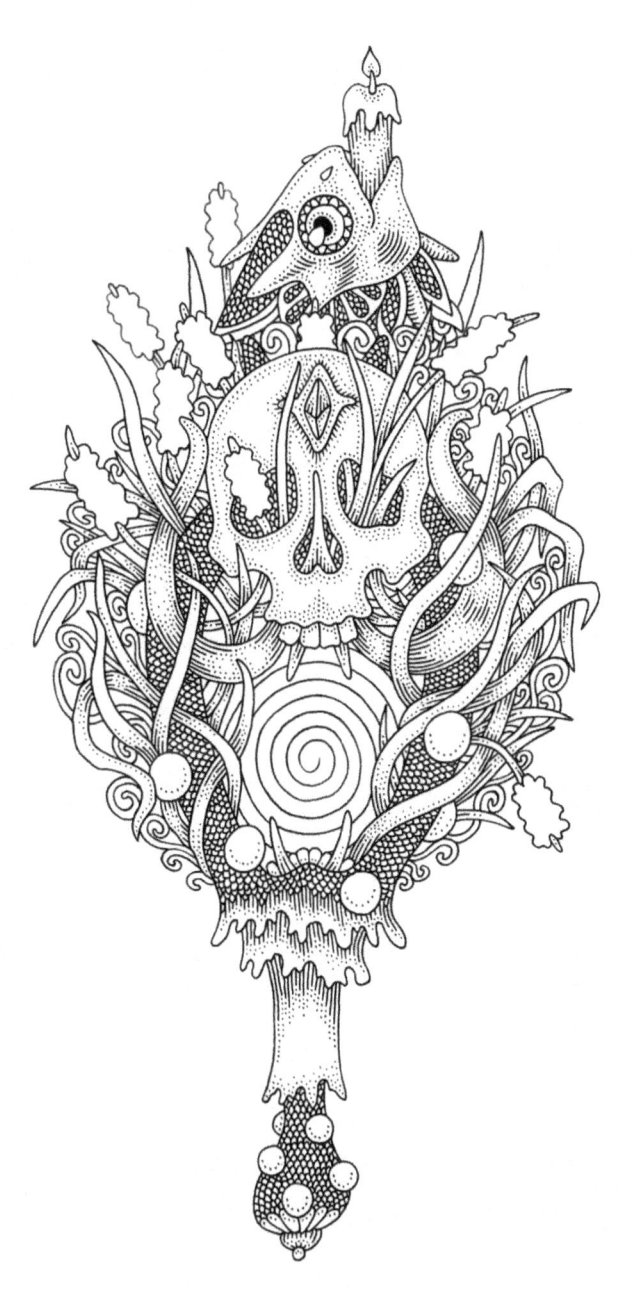

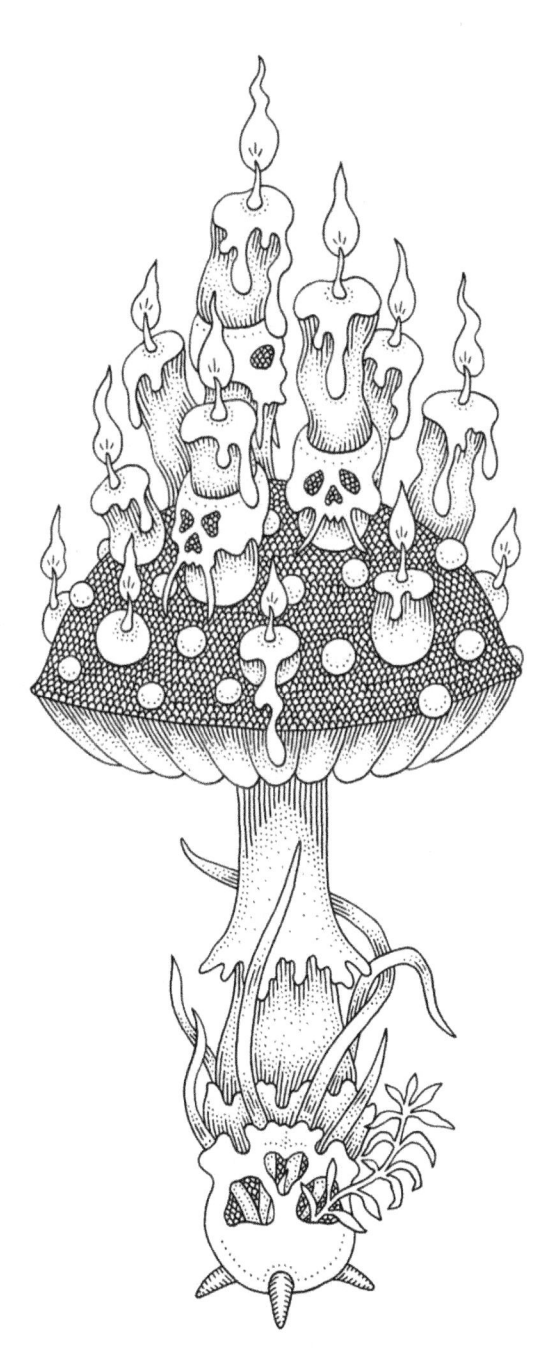

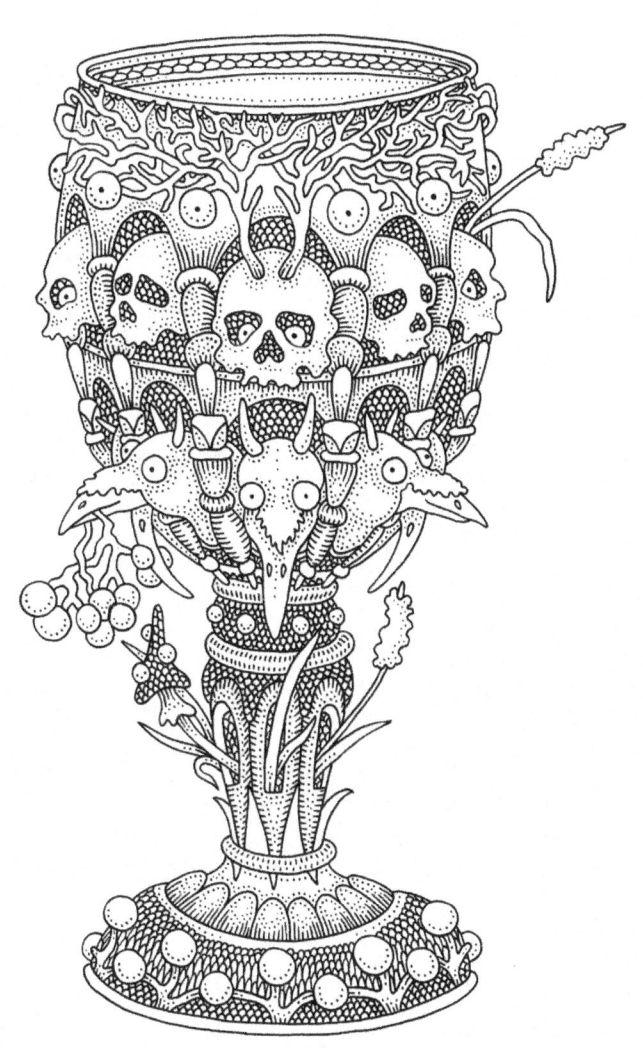

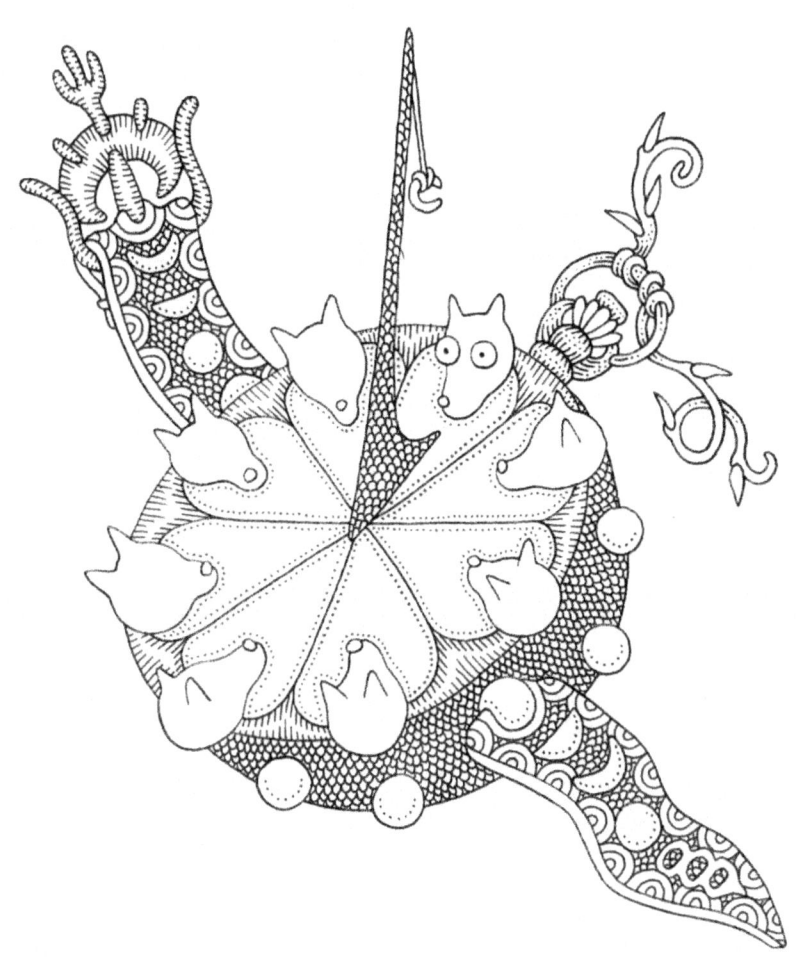

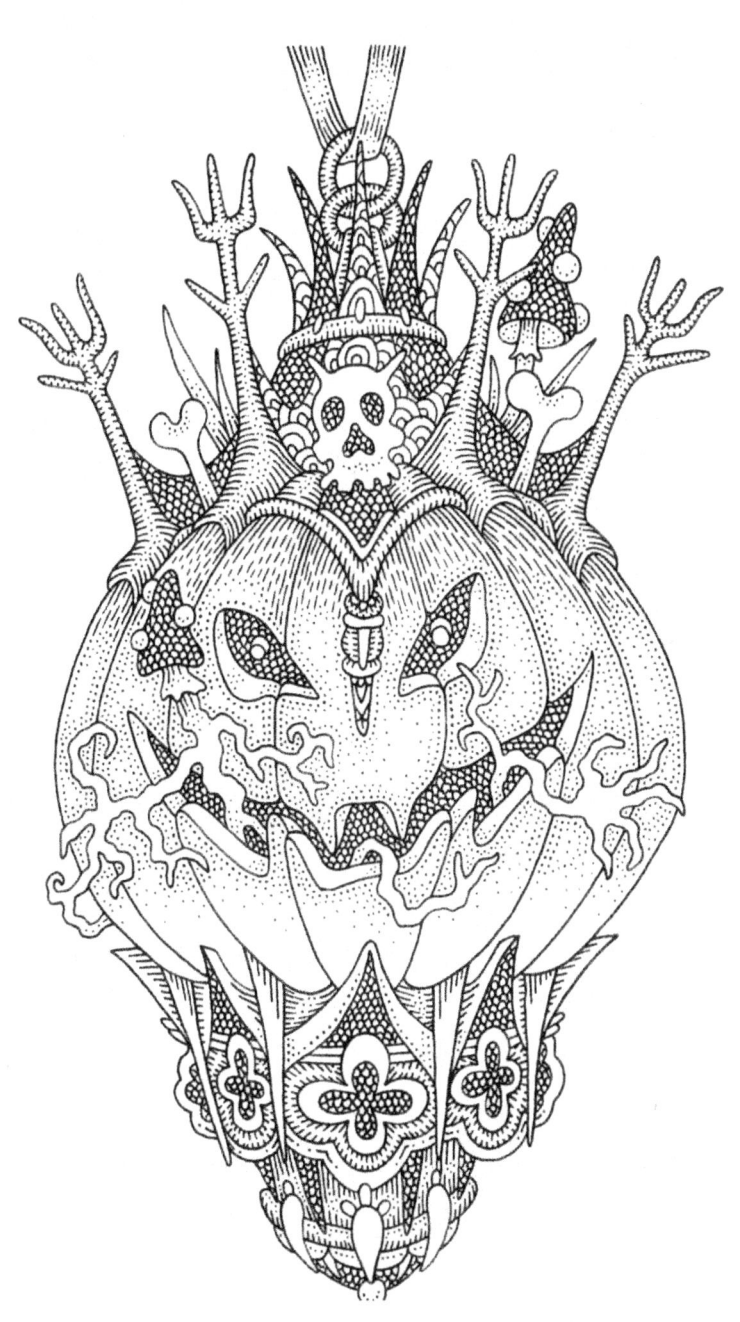

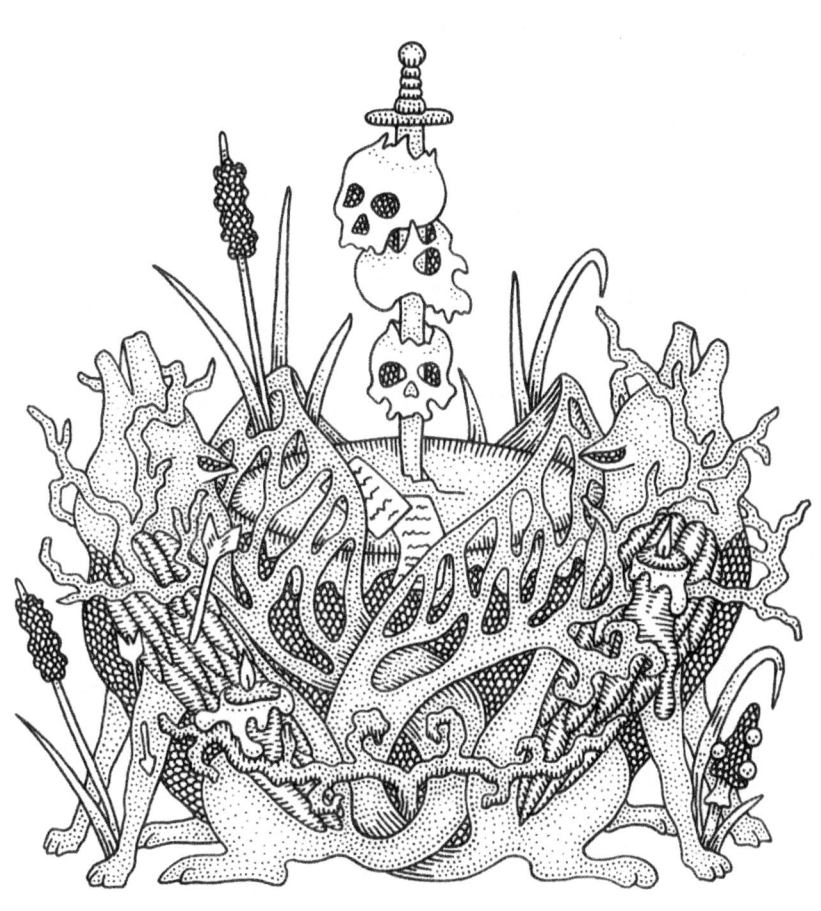

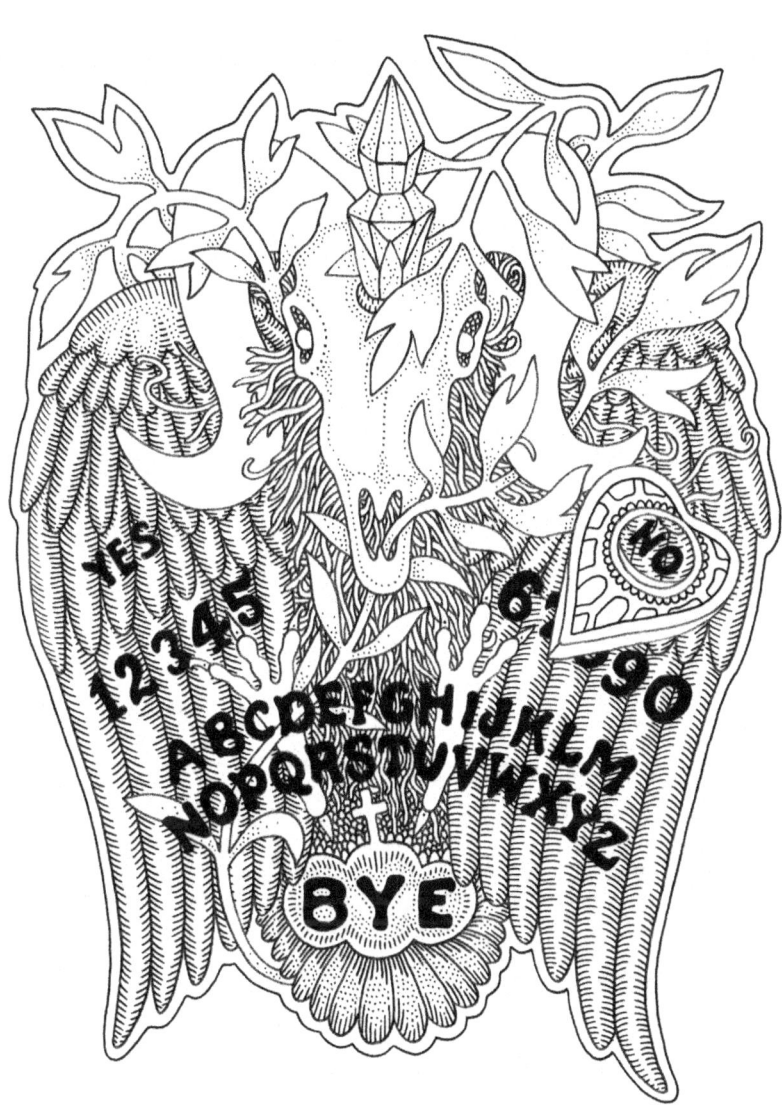

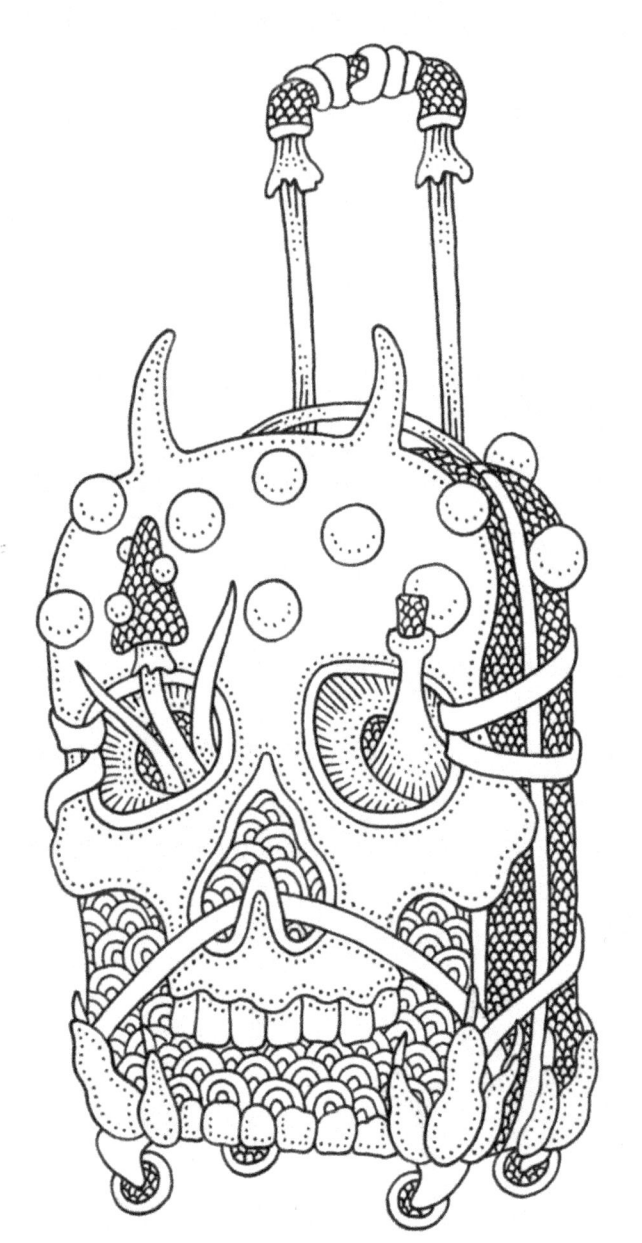

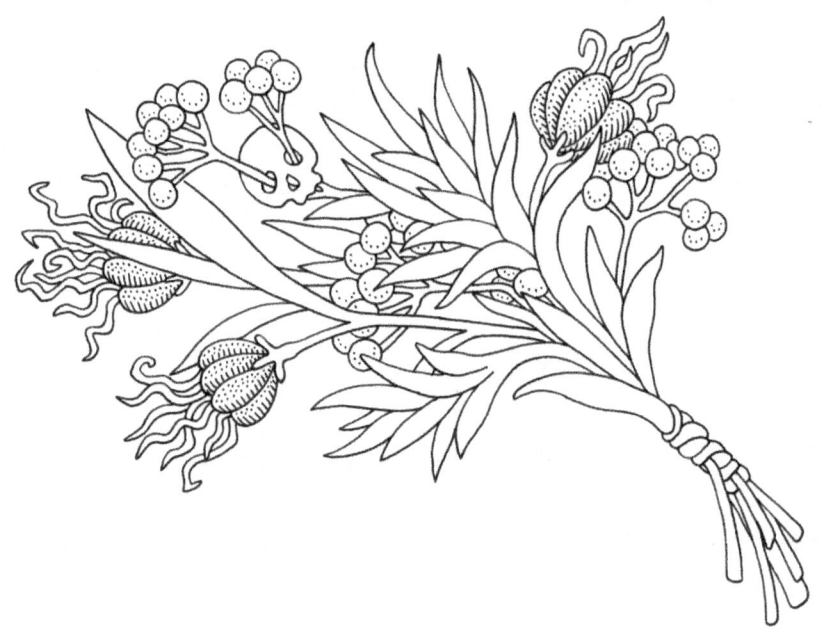

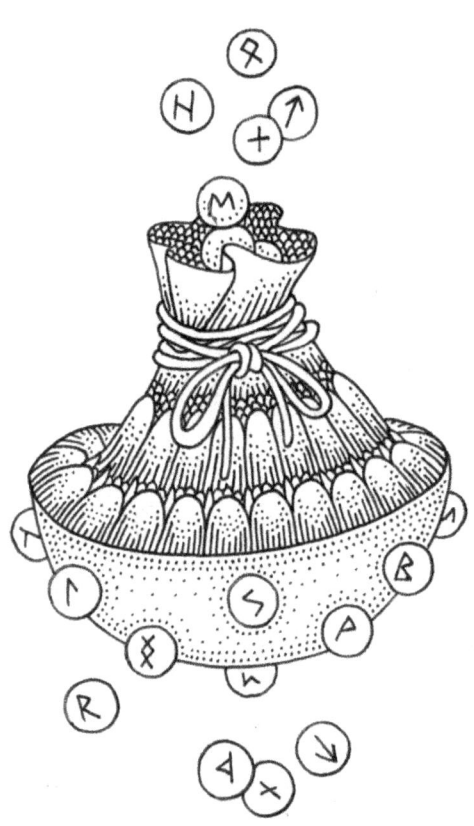

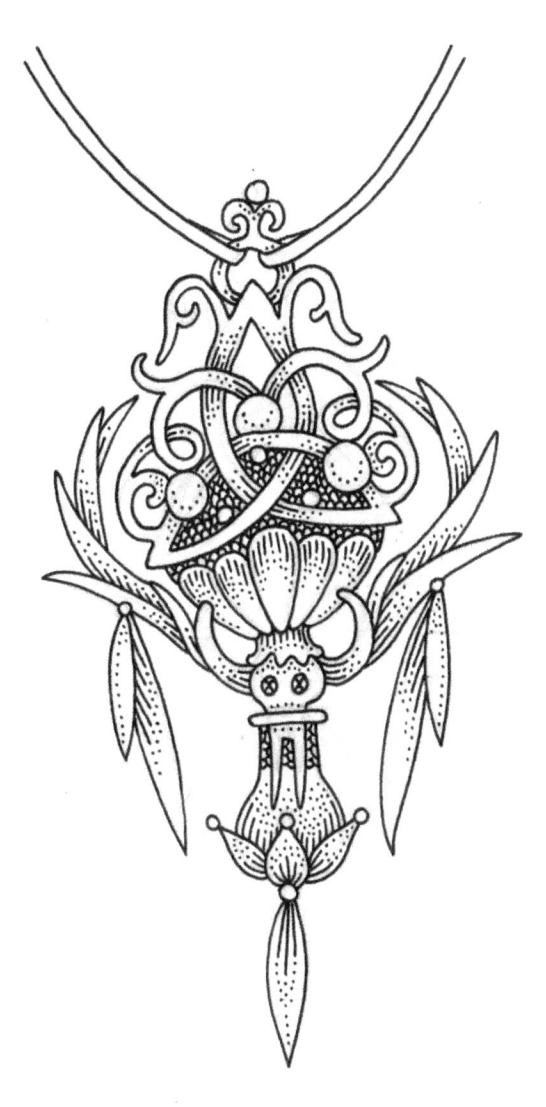

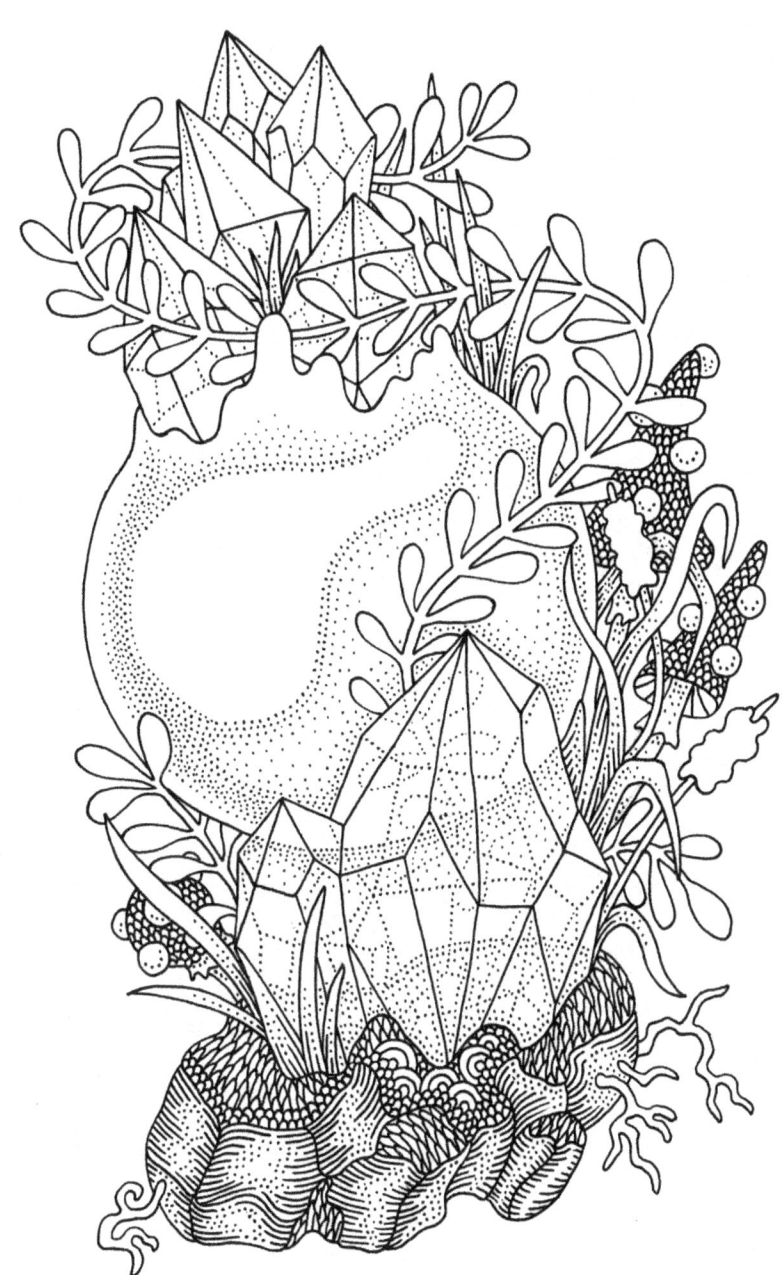

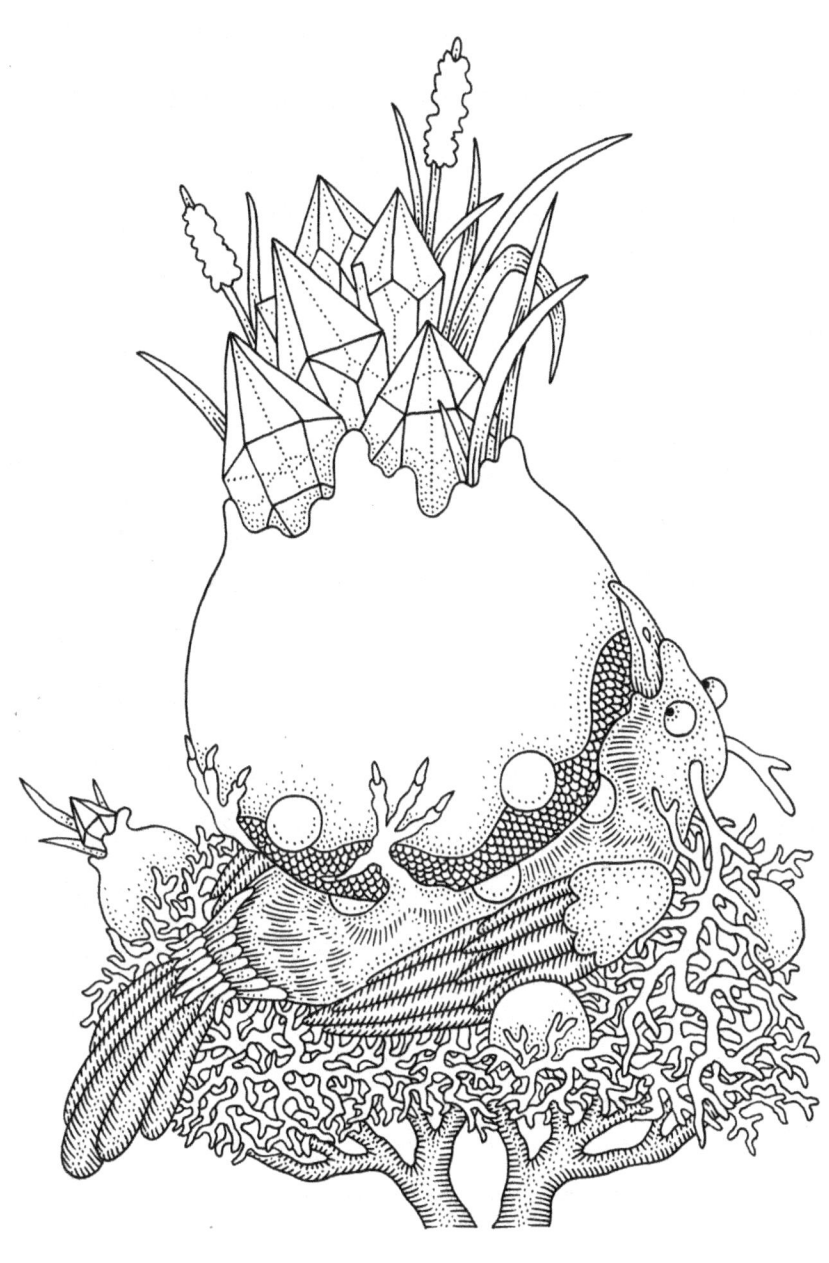

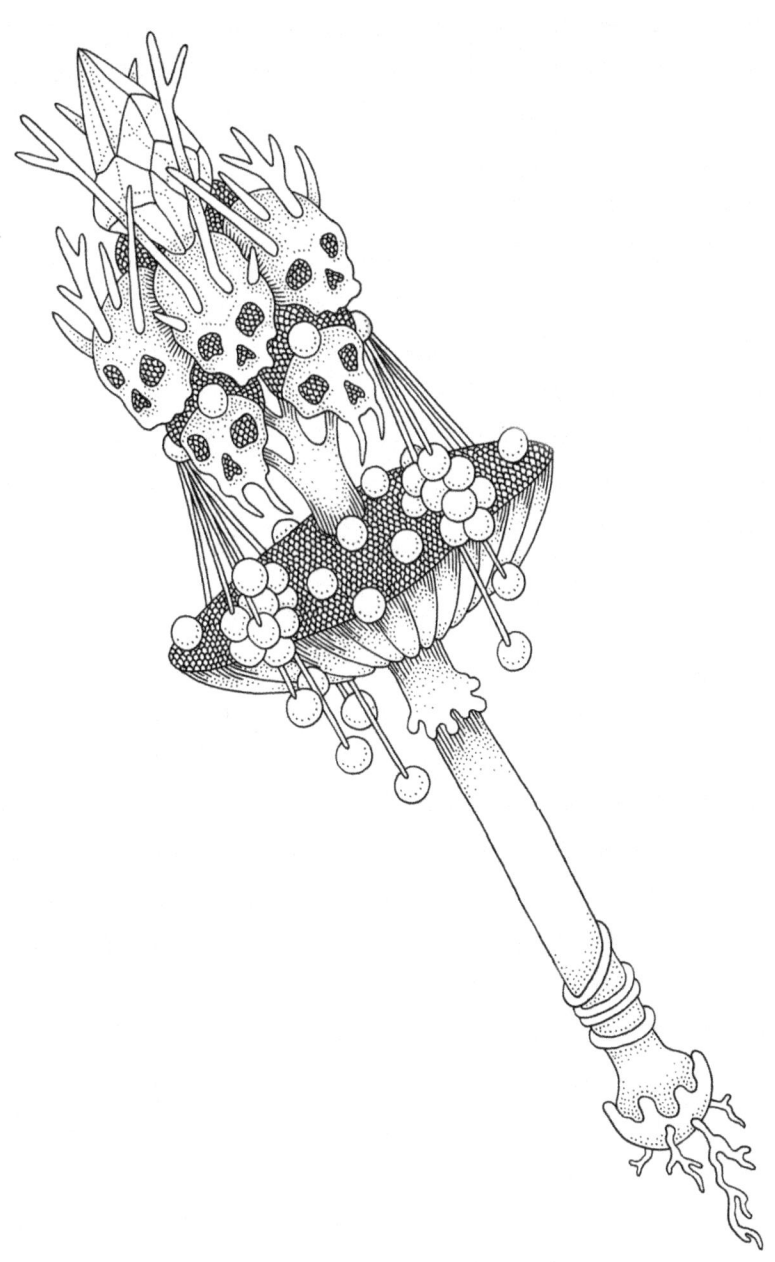

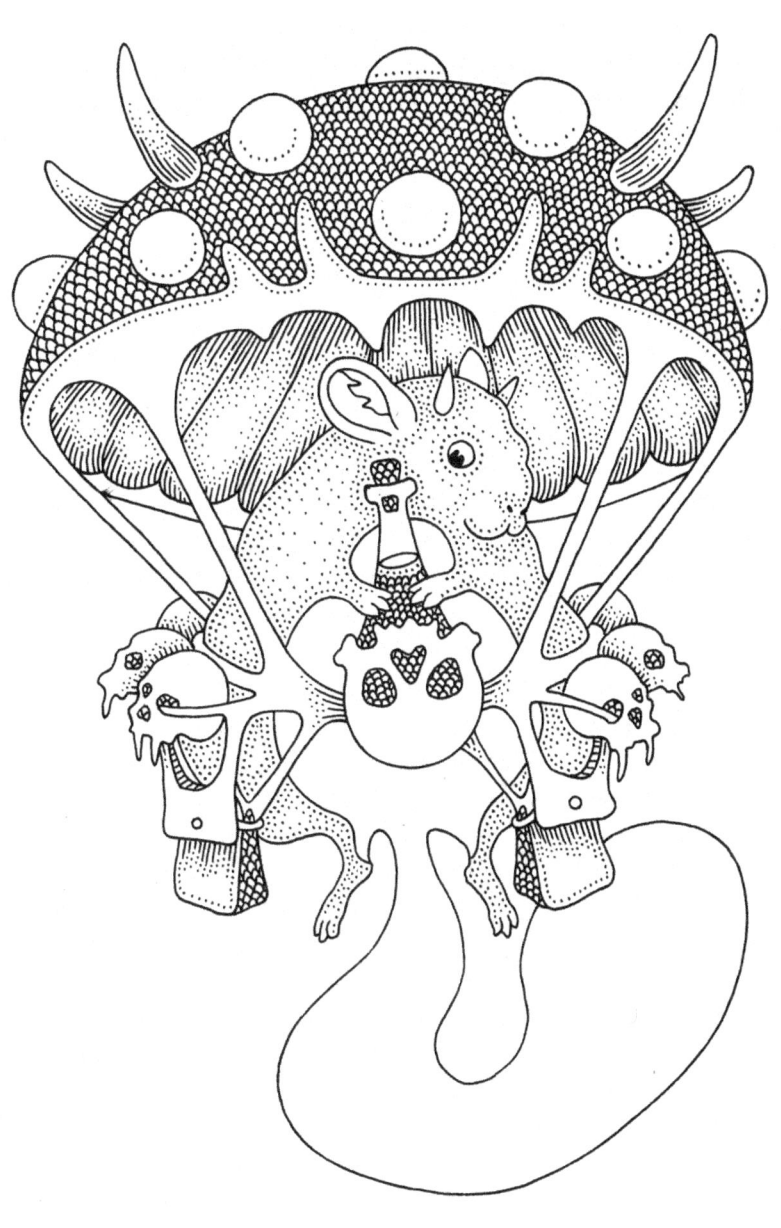

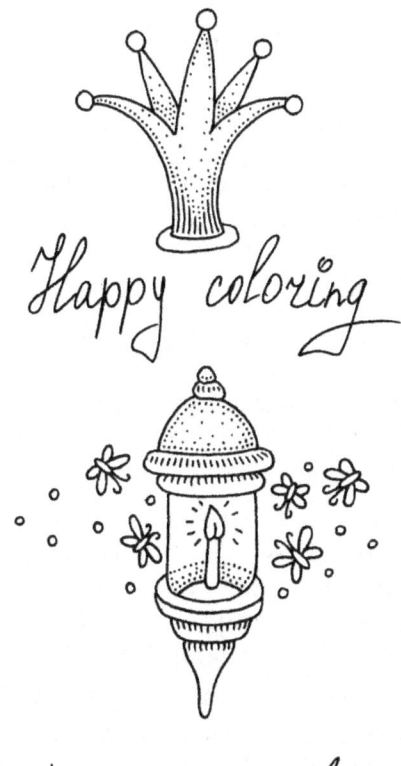

Happy coloring

Thank you for choosing
my coloring book!

Olya

Olga Goloveshkina is a freelance artist and illustrator based in Moscow, Russia.

Olga Goloveshkina is a freelance artist and illustrator based in Moscow, Russia.

Education:
Moscow State Humanities University (History Faculty)
Institute of Business and Design (Graphic Design)

She is an author and illustrator coloring books for adults:
1. "The wind carries flowers"/"Veter unosit tsvety" (in Russian, 2015),
2. "Fox travel: Coloring book" (in English, 2016),
3. "Mounts" (in English, 2016),
4. "Mounts 2" (in English, 2016),
5. "Enchanted horses" (in English, 2016),
6. "Horse and Architecture" (in English, 2016),
7. "Alice in Wonderland Coloring Book" (in English, 2017),
8. "Mounts 3" zodiac coloring book (in English, 2017),
9. "Mounts 4" Halloween coloring book (in English, 2017),
10. "Mounts 5" Christmas coloring book (in English, 2017),
11. "The queens. Monsters. Werewolves. Goddesses."Coloring book" (in English, 2018),
12. "Chinchilla Art Journal Coloring Book" (in English, 2018),
13. "Chinchillum botanicum. Coloring book" (in English, 2018),
14. "Gray Gray Wolf: Tsarevitch Ivan, the Firebird and the Gray Wolf. A Russian Folk Story. Graphic novel. Coloring book." (in English, 2018),
15. "Find the skull. Halloween coloring book" (in English, 2019).

Exhibitions:
"ArtForPlanetFest" WWF Russia, Moscow 2018
"ArtForPlanetFest" WWF Russia, Moscow 2019

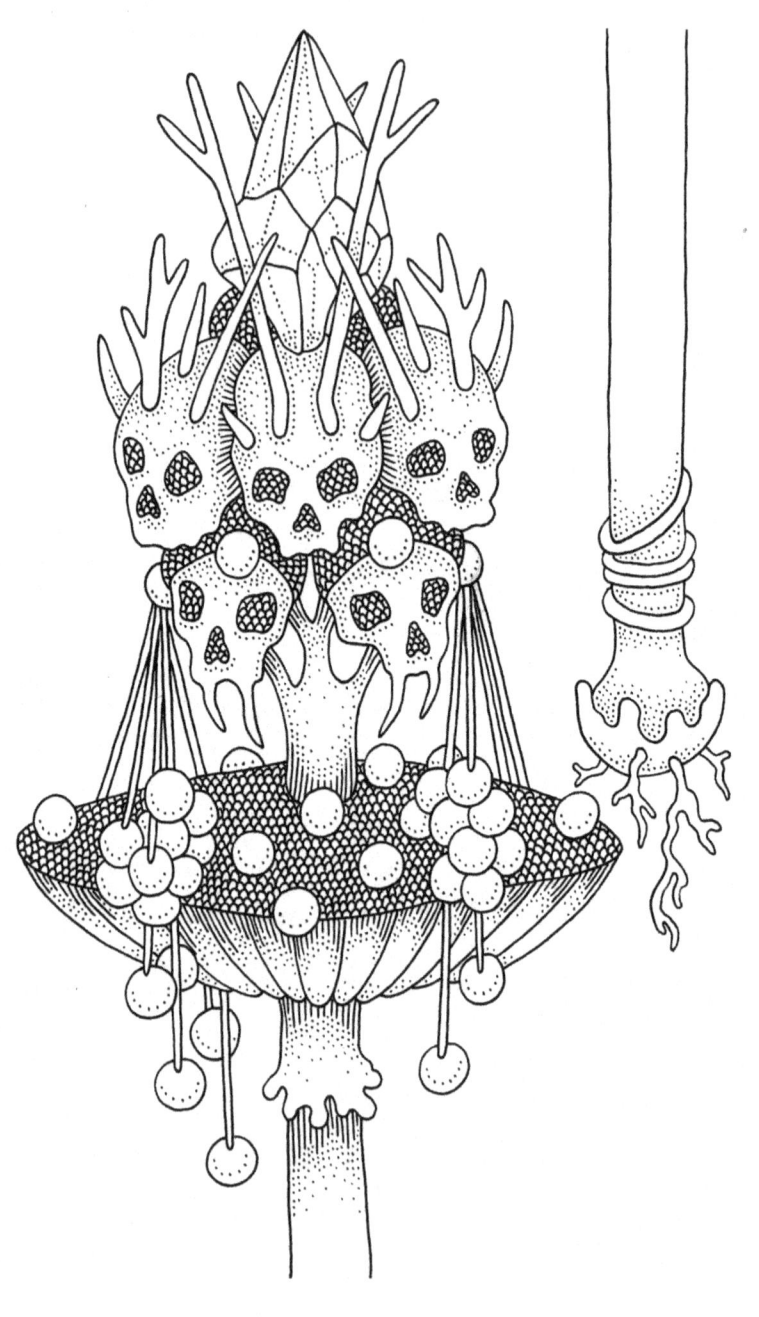

www.ingramcontent.com/pod-product-compliance
Lightning Source LLC
Chambersburg PA
CBHW070342220526
45467CB00001B/219